MW01308976

Introduction

I remember the first time I was admitted to the psych ward. I was young, attending college at Stanford, not even twenty years old yet. I told the nurses in the emergency room that I had two plans to kill myself. What I didn't tell them was that I'd also attempted to drive my car off the side of a California cliff – no plan that time, just an impulse after the voices in my head had gotten so obnoxiously loud I could barely breathe. I just needed to make them stop. But I kept that secret to myself; I'd seen enough movies to know what they did to people who let the voices in their head win in the end. They locked me up anyway. I don't know what I expected them to do; I was a danger to myself – clearly! And I was afraid. Very afraid. The grey walls of the hospital room closed in on me as my arms flailed and my legs kicked the hard floor beneath me. I slid down my Mother's leg and tantrummed like a toddler as they pulled me away from her to take me to the psychiatric ward. I yelled at her, "Stay! If you love me, you won't leave me here!" Those words echoed through the halls. I tried to etch her face in my mind as if I would somehow forget. It wasn't long before I was in my room, alone, under suicide watch, diagnosed with severe acute clinical depression. Bipolar disorder and anxiety joined the team later.

I didn't forget my Mom. Not that day or the next. I didn't forget anyone, or anything, for that matter. But I did remember… I remembered me. And the me I remembered was finally free. See, when I was officially diagnosed, I didn't feel crippled anymore. Or disabled. I felt liberated somehow. This diagnosis gave me something to hold on to, to explore, to wrap my heart around. Being able to say, "Ohhhhhh okay, so that's what this thing is," was freeing. It wasn't about me being crazy anymore, which is how I felt pretty much every day. Instead of existing in confusion, I could begin exploring my diagnosis and working my recovery plan. It became an extended exercise in getting to know me, understand me, and love me through this new lens. And it's been a pretty fascinating, and often exhausting, process. Some people never get the opportunity to truly explore who they are, you know, at their core. I'm still in gratitude around it all. And I'm still learning. But I've been able to figure out a few life-saving things along the way.

Many years after my second - and final - visit to the psych ward, I took time to design a Mental Fitness Plan that worked for me. I'd been in and out of therapy – group therapy, cognitive therapy, art therapy… - and I'd tried every cocktail of meds under the sun for depression, bipolar disorder, psychosis, and anxiety. But the ten steps in my Mental Fitness Plan have been revolutionary in my approach to living a fulfilling, *extra*-ordinary life.

I've used my time to find what works best for me as I continue to live with and manage my mental health. People always ask me how I've been able to graduate from Stanford, or perform as a Chicago Bulls cheerleader, or even graduate with an MBA and publish books with Random House. The answer is simple: my Mental Fitness Plan! This ten-step plan keeps me balanced and centered, while also building in time for me to be reflective and still. My goal for you is to design your own Mental Fitness Plan by prioritizing the ten steps found in this workbook. I want you to mark up these pages with words and drawings and pictures and journal entries. This is YOUR MENTAL FITNESS PLAN. And as you work through the book, remember to be patient with yourself. Trust the process. And always – and I mean always - reward yourself. That's my favorite part. Plus, you're super worth it!

The Mental Fitness Plan saved my life and helped me rediscover *My Happy*. Spoiler Alert: it was inside me all along. And by consistently working the ten steps of my plan, the process ultimately gives me permission to live each day fully – present in every moment. I wish the same for you.

Please know that I love you – always have, always will.
And I don't have to know you to love you.

Erika

Let's go find your Happy…

GRATITUDE

As you move forward to find your happy, remember that you are already starting from a place of abundance and prosperity.

My family:

1. ____________________
2. ____________________
3. ____________________

My friends:

1. ____________________
2. ____________________
3. ____________________

My talents:

1. ____________________
2. ____________________
3. ____________________

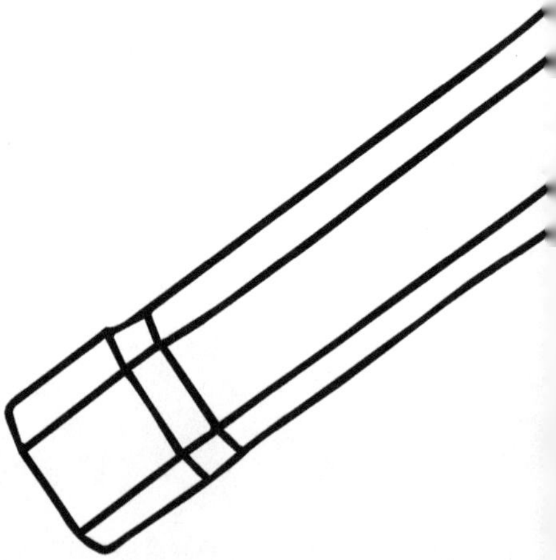

My mentors & teachers:

1.
2.
3.

I am GREATful for...

One

YOUR VIP SUPPORT SQUAD

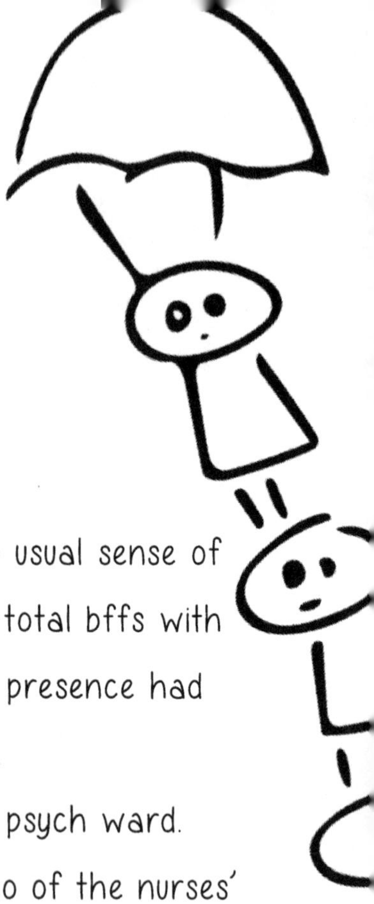

I remember being in the hospital psychiatric ward, feeling my usual sense of overwhelming hopelessness and emptiness, two symptoms that are total bffs with major depression. These feelings weren't new to me; in fact, their presence had become as normal and dependable as my inability to reclaim my life.

I was almost twenty years old and it was my first time in a psych ward. I could hear the patter of feet breezing past my door and the echo of the nurses' voices yelling something about visiting hours. I pulled myself from the twin bed and trudged into the group area to join the others. There was a quiet excitement in the air. And that's when I saw her, the captain of my Support Squad, (aka Mom). She was the first person through the big double doors with tears in her eyes and open arms.

I looked at the girl next to me and said, "Told you she'd be the first one here." I often wondered if she'd slept outside in the car.

My Dad sauntered in behind her, his Fedora hat in hand, anxious to see that his baby girl was okay. He was the co-captain of my Support Squad. My Grandma and my best friends, along with other family members, had always been elite members of my Support Squad too.

I take membership in my Squad very seriously. *Everyone should.*

Every year, several spots on my Support Squad were held just for a special group of sister girlfriends who championed my journey. They were the Girl Scout crew, girls and their moms who'd been in my lil world for over fifteen years. We'd built campfires, pitched tents, and traded secrets into the twilight hours of too many summer nights to count. And now, as they visited me in the psych ward and the many days and nights that followed, they just couldn't make sense of me being suicidal or depressed. After all, "What did she have to be depressed about?" they asked themselves, each other, and me all too often. But it was okay that they didn't get what was happening inside my brain. It was okay that they'd never experienced the kind of brain pain that decorated my truth. And it was definitely okay that they had never experienced the kind of piercing emptiness that had become familiar to me. What mattered was they were there -- confused, yes, and saddened by my affect and this mysterious internal struggle that had seemingly taken over the Erika they once knew. THEY WERE THERE, nonetheless. Even when they couldn't find the words to soothe me, their presence reassured me that I was never alone, even though I felt overwhelmingly lonely. They definitely earned their VIP spots on my Support Squad.

Everyone needs a Support Squad, especially when they're struggling with mental health challenges. Having others you can trust and rely on to be there when you can't be there for yourself not only speeds up the learning and recovery process, but it can also be incredibly healing.

WRITE YOUR NAME HERE

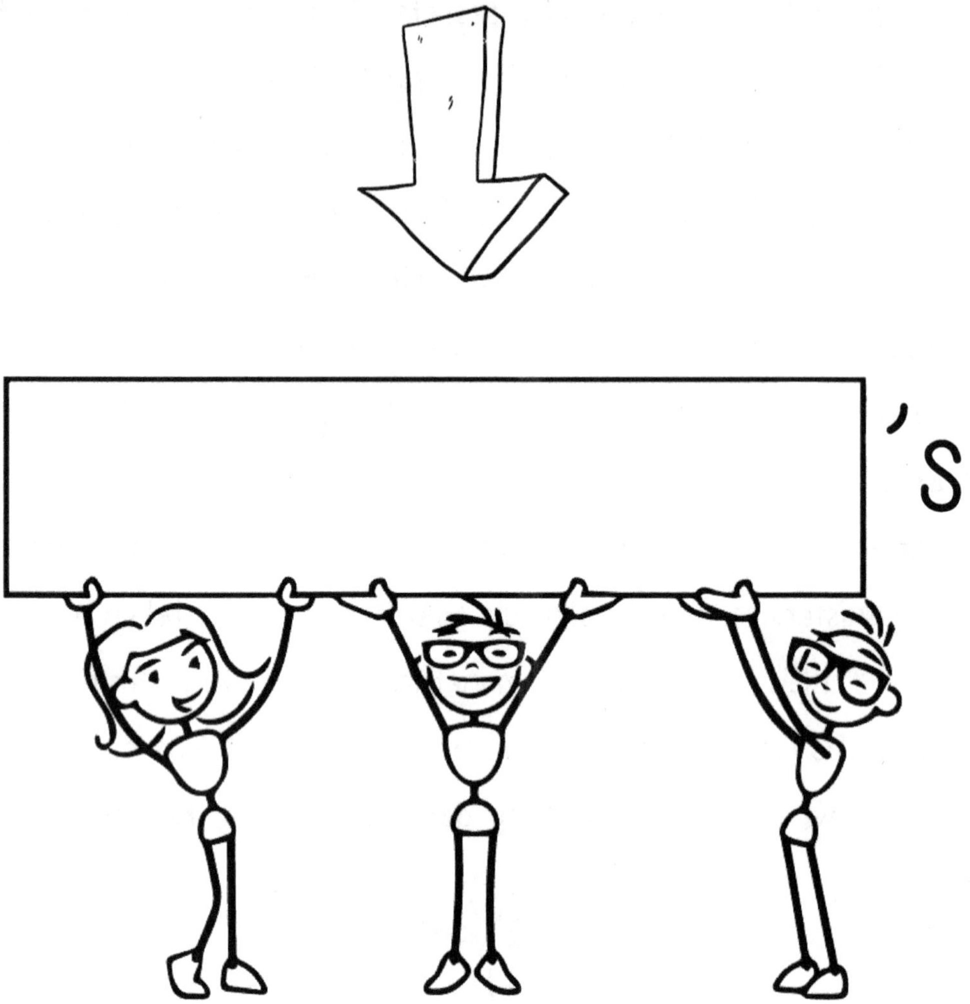
’s

Support Squad

Who should be in your Support Squad?

Support Squad candidates can be parents, family members, friends, your therapist, doctors, or even pets (more on that later). There are some rules or requirements to consider as you audition or quietly interview people to join your exclusive Support Squad.

A good support squad avoids phrases like...

"SNAP OUT OF IT!" and **"GET OVER IT!"** or **"JUST SHAKE IT OFF!"**

RULES

Support Squad Members:

1. They must be trustworthy.
2. They must make you feel respected and safe.
3. They must listen to you without judgment and criticism. Yes, this is a must, but keep in mind that it can also be taught, especially to those who want to learn how to support you even when they disagree or don't understand your thoughts or feelings.
4. They must be positive, steering clear of negativity and cynicism -- you have enough of that happening on your own.

Your Support Squad should...

NEVER MAKE YOU FEEL ANXIOUS OR TO BLAME FOR YOUR MENTAL HEALTH CHALLENGES.

It's a good idea to include a mental health peer group in your Support Squad! When we share experiences, it connects us. It also gives us hope and reassurance that we can get through it. Our resident teacher, Professor Happy, teaches us that having a SUPPORT SQUAD can help ease depression.

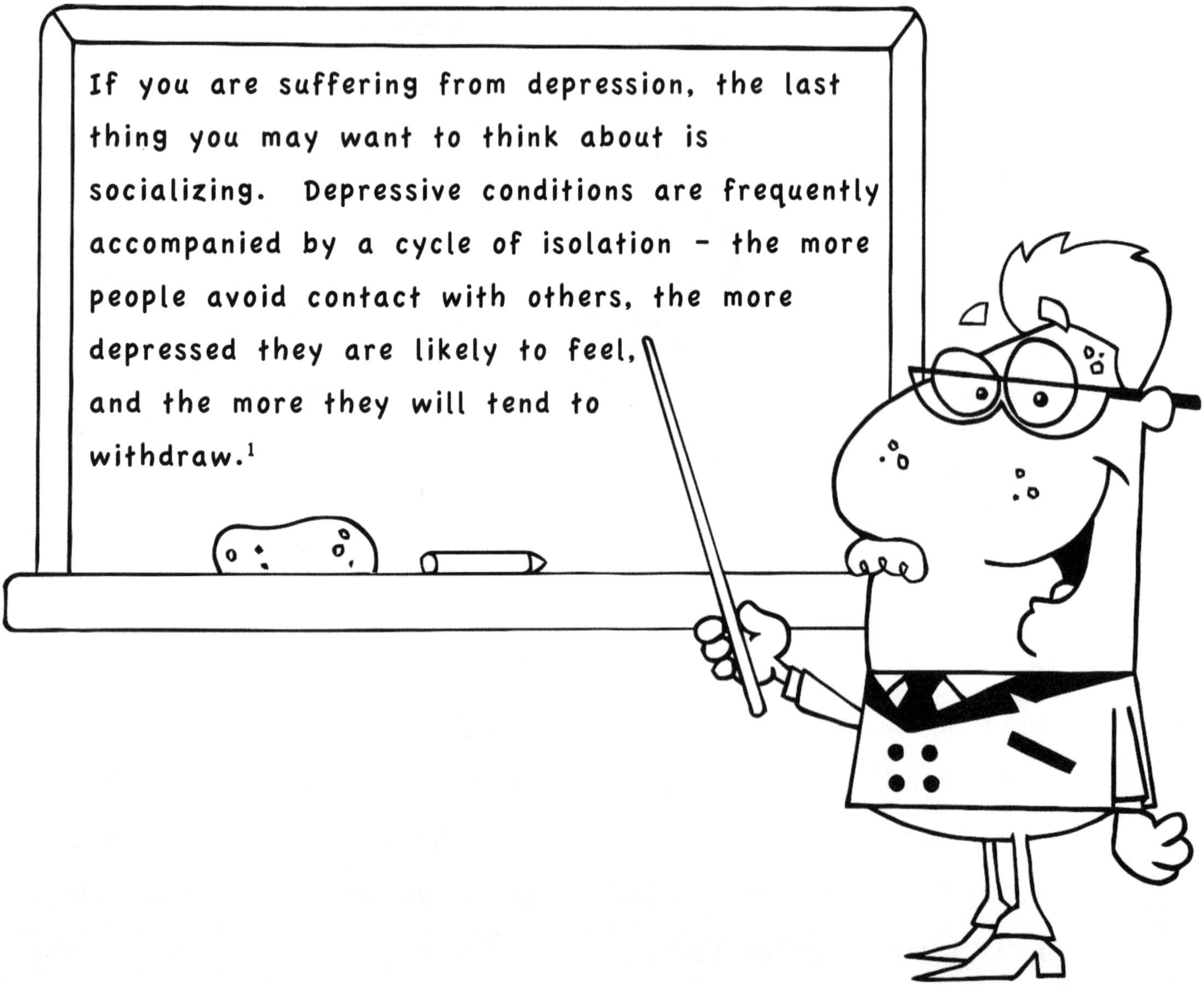
If you are suffering from depression, the last thing you may want to think about is socializing. Depressive conditions are frequently accompanied by a cycle of isolation - the more people avoid contact with others, the more depressed they are likely to feel, and the more they will tend to withdraw.[1]

BUILD YOUR VERY IMPORTANT PERSON SUPPORT SQUAD

Remember, choose people that make you feel supported and loved. Use the BOX OF FEELINGS below to guide you.

You get to choose... IT'S YOUR VIP SQUAD!

Name	How do they make me feel?
1. ____________	____________________
2. ____________	____________________
3. ____________	____________________
4. ____________	____________________
5. ____________	____________________

Valued Seen Honored Affirmed Trusted

Respected Proud Brave Important Cherished

Grateful Whole Loyal Peaceful Strong Secure

Happy Purposeful Upbeat Trustworthy Encouraged

Loved Protected Safe Excited Attractive

Supported Powerful Adored Loved Free

Successful Fun Helpful Inspired

color me

BOOK YOUR SUPPORT SQUAD!

3 Activities YOU enjoy and the best SQUAD member for them:

Activity: *Exercise*

1. *Squad Member: Monica*
2. *Squad Member: Lauren*
3. *Squad Member: Amber*

Activity: ______

1. *Squad Member:* ______
2. *Squad Member:* ______
3. *Squad Member:* ______

Activity: ______

1. *Squad Member:* ______
2. *Squad Member:* ______
3. *Squad Member:* ______

Activity: ______

1. *Squad Member:* ______
2. *Squad Member:* ______
3. *Squad Member:* ______

LET'S SET THE DATE!

Contact each Support Squad member and get booked. They should be people with whom you enjoy doing activities, but your Support Squad should also hold you accountable and make sure you stay committed to the activity.

Consider making weekly plans.

If you like exercising on Mondays when you have a fresh start to your week, book squad members who will enjoy exercising too, like Monica and/or Lauren.

MONDAY: *Monica and Lauren*

Activity: *2-4pm*

Time: *Exercise – Bike riding at the lake*

Note: *Lauren has piano practice so she'll be late. Monica is going to bring the bottled water.*

And then on Tuesdays, book your favorite mall Squad to shop.

I know it can be hard when you're not feeling your best, especially since that's when it takes the most effort to reach out. But just remember, THAT'S WHEN YOU REALLY NEED TO BOOK YOUR SUPPORT SQUAD. Booking yourself to hang out under the covers every day won't help you find YOUR HAPPY!

Book your week...
WITH YOUR SUPPORT SQUAD!

MONDAY: ____________________

Activity: ____________________

Time: ____________________

Note: ____________________

TUESDAY: ____________________

Activity: ____________________

Time: ____________________

Note: ____________________

WEDNESDAY: ____________________

Activity: ____________________

Time: ____________________

Note: ____________________

THURSDAY:

Activity:

Time:

Note:

FRIDAY:

Activity:

Time:

Note:

SATURDAY:

Activity:

Time:

Note:

SUNDAY:

Activity:

Time:

Note:

How do you feel about...

BUILDING YOUR SUPPORT SQUAD AND BOOKING THEM?

I feel...

I'm excited about...

I'm nervous about...

Two

THERAPY

Just like dating...

do you like me?
yes
no
maybe

My mother was my first therapist.

If that sounds dysfunctional and slightly unorthodox, it was. My Mom is a practicing therapist, and while she truly is the bee's knees for her clients, she wasn't a good fit for me. I decided that at the mature age of 8 after jumping out of my classroom window in an attempt to run away from the nuns. Mom was too furious (and utterly embarrassed) to empathize with the exact motivation behind my rebellious behavior. Luckily, she handed me over to one of her colleagues and I was off to the races, ready to have someone explain why the runaway in me kept trying to escape my life. (B.T.Dubs, I ran away from home about once a month and tried to escape moving vehicles as well.)

My new therapist took a different, more effective approach with me than my mother, mainly because she didn't have to lock my door from the outside and explain to everyone why they needed to keep a close eye on me whenever she dropped me off somewhere. The new therapist and I were a hit from the start, and I've been in and out of therapy ever since. And while I know that therapy saved my life and helped me find new ways of dealing with the escape artist living inside me, I also know that there isn't always a simple, linear route to finding the right therapist.

Did you know...

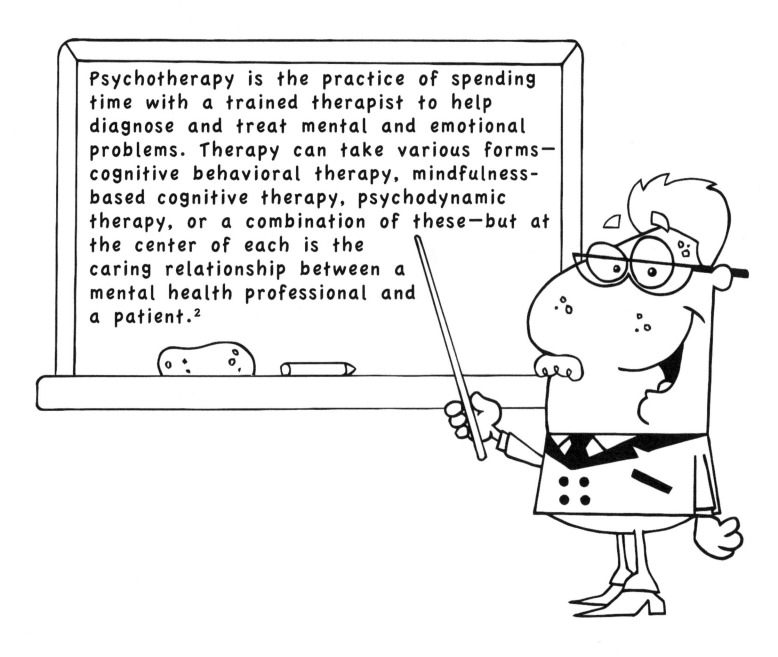

Psychotherapy is the practice of spending time with a trained therapist to help diagnose and treat mental and emotional problems. Therapy can take various forms—cognitive behavioral therapy, mindfulness-based cognitive therapy, psychodynamic therapy, or a combination of these—but at the center of each is the caring relationship between a mental health professional and a patient.[2]

Just like dating …

You have to try on a few different personalities in order to find

THE BEST FIT.

THERAPY WANTS TO KNOW **HOW YOU FEEL ABOUT IT…**

- ☐ I love it. I have a great relationship with my therapist.
- ☐ I've been to a few casual sessions, but nothing too serious.
- ☐ Nah, I'm not that into it.

Finding the right therapist is like *finding your soul mate.* FAREAL.

The right therapist can add significant value and improve your life. But if you allow yourself to stay with the wrong one past the first or second date, they can make your life more complicated, painful, and harder to manage than before you met them. And, well, that defeats the purpose.

Therapy-ing can be a struggle, just like dating. You have to talk on the telephone to interview them, and then after you've built up the courage to go on the dreaded "first date" and meet them face-to-face, you have to assess your time together and decide if the person is a good match for you and worth seeing again. Then if it isn't a good match, you have to start the process all over again. It can seem tedious, but it's worth it. You're worth it. And remember, you're in control. Like I said, therapy saved my life. It can help you too and put you on the path to finding your happy.

So let's get you matched for your...

Happily ever after

Step-By-Step

THERAPY MATCHMAKER

First... Get several referrals – at least 5 - from your Support Squad. Referrals can come from friends and family, coworkers, online searches in your area, or from your primary care physician and/or insurance provider. Keep a running list - with notes - so you can keep track of your progress.

Name: ______________ Phone: ______________

Website: ______________ Notes: ______________

____

____

Name: ______________ Phone: ______________

Website: ______________ Notes: ______________

____

____

Name: ______________________ Phone: ______________________

Website: ______________________ Notes: ______________________

Name: ______________________ Phone: ______________________

Website: ______________________ Notes: ______________________

Name: ______________________ Phone: ______________________

Website: ______________________ Notes: ______________________

What are my needs?

Identify your needs before you make the big call to any of your prospective therapists.

When I started therapy again after a suicidal attempt that I'd kept secret, I knew I needed help with getting the toxic, stinkin' thinkin' in my head to stop. The doctors had officially diagnosed me with major depression and I even found myself admitting to them that I had two plans to kill myself; yes, I was a true overachiever. Over time, though, therapy helped me reframe my negative thoughts, and ultimately, I was able to move past victimization toward empowerment - a critical step in my journey to finding my happy.

It's okay if you aren't sure of your exact needs.

A good therapist will be able to help you clarify them.

Clarification is important because it is essential that you and your therapist are both clear about the direction of your time together and your goals.

AREAS YOU MAY WANT TO ADDRESS WITH YOUR THERAPIST:

Your family

Your childhood

Your relationship(s)

What's happening in your life right now

The negative thoughts you're having

Self-harm or Suicidal thoughts

Use the sentence starters to help you clarify your needs before you call.

B
E
F
O
R
E

Y
O
U

C
A
L
L

I would like to talk with a therapist about ______________________

I've been struggling in my every day life with ______________________

Lately, I've been constantly thinking about ______________________

I've been stuck ______________________

I need strategies to help me ______________________

THE BIG FIRST CALL

Now, it's TIME TO CALL each of the therapists on your list. And just like a date, it's time to evaluate them and see if they work for YOU. YOU ARE THE STAR, and don't you forget it!

And just like you should be direct and ask potential dating mates if they're married, you should be direct with the therapists while you have them on the phone.

FIRST CALL QUESTIONS FOR THE THERAPIST:

1. What are your specialties?
2. I'm having issues in my relationship, how would you help me?
3. What are three of your strengths as a therapist?
4. What are a few of your weaknesses as a therapist?
5. What would a typical therapy session look like?
6. Have you ever been in therapy?
   ♥This one is like asking them have they ever been in a relationship before? If they haven't, they may not be the best person to help you with yours.

Make sure you pick the therapist that makes you feel comfortable and relaxed.

Time for **THE BIG DATE**

Remember, you're in control. They need to impress you with their ability to help you. And if they can't, you move on to the next one. If the relationship seems doomed from the start, you should ALWAYS LEAVE.

...

The search is about finding your best match!

POST-DATE REFLECTION

Once you meet your new therapist, make sure it's a good fit for you. Consider how your therapist makes you feel. It should be a positive experience.

POSITIVE:

Understood
Challenged
Calm
Valued
Happy
Respected
Powerful
Supported
Confident
Hopeful
Assured
Confident
Strong
Relaxed
Proud
Ready
Focused

NEGATIVE:

Criticized
Judged
Anxious
Worthless
Sad
Abused
Small
Empty
Hopeless
Shame
Doubt
Despair
Frustration
Grief
Guilt
Frightened
Ashamed

REFLECTION JOURNAL

At the beginning of the session, I felt

In the middle of the session, I felt

At the end of the session, I felt

Right now, I feel

It was really good to talk to my therapist about

If I decide to stick with this therapist, in our next session I'd like to talk more about

Will I see this therapist again?

- [ ] YES
- [ ] NO

If yes, when?

DATE:

TIME:

LOCATION:

• Remember, therapy is a commitment, not a quick fix. Keep your appointments. And if it isn't working out, start over!

Three

HEALTHY BELLIES

CLEAN EATS

I wore several dietary lifestyle t-shirts (meatatarian, pescatarian, vegetarian, etc.) before becoming a vegan. Yep, that's right, I'm an out and proud vegan – no meat or dairy for me. And pinky swear, it's one of the best things I've done for my body and for my brain. I don't have to worry about being lactose intolerant or having a bloated, crampy

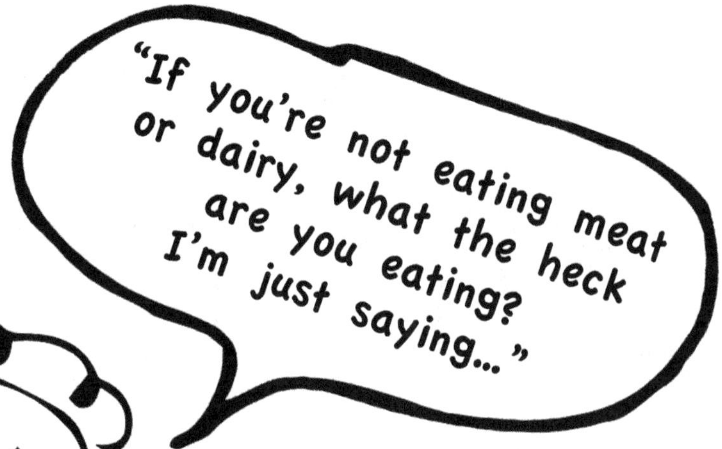
"If you're not eating meat or dairy, what the heck are you eating? I'm just saying..."

tummy after I enjoy my food. My brain doesn't live in a thick fog anymore either; it gets clean fuel and it's had a huge impact on my moods and my overall physical and mental health.

Now you might be wondering what can a vegan eat if not dairy or meat? No worries, I get that question all the time.

When I was relatively new to being a vegan (a plant-based diet with no animals or dairy), my choices were limited when I didn't cook. And while I lived in Manhattan with more vegan food choices than most cities, I remember being on book tour and realizing that salad - with a side of salad - pretty much summed up my menu options everywhere else I went. Luckily, that's changing - and fast.

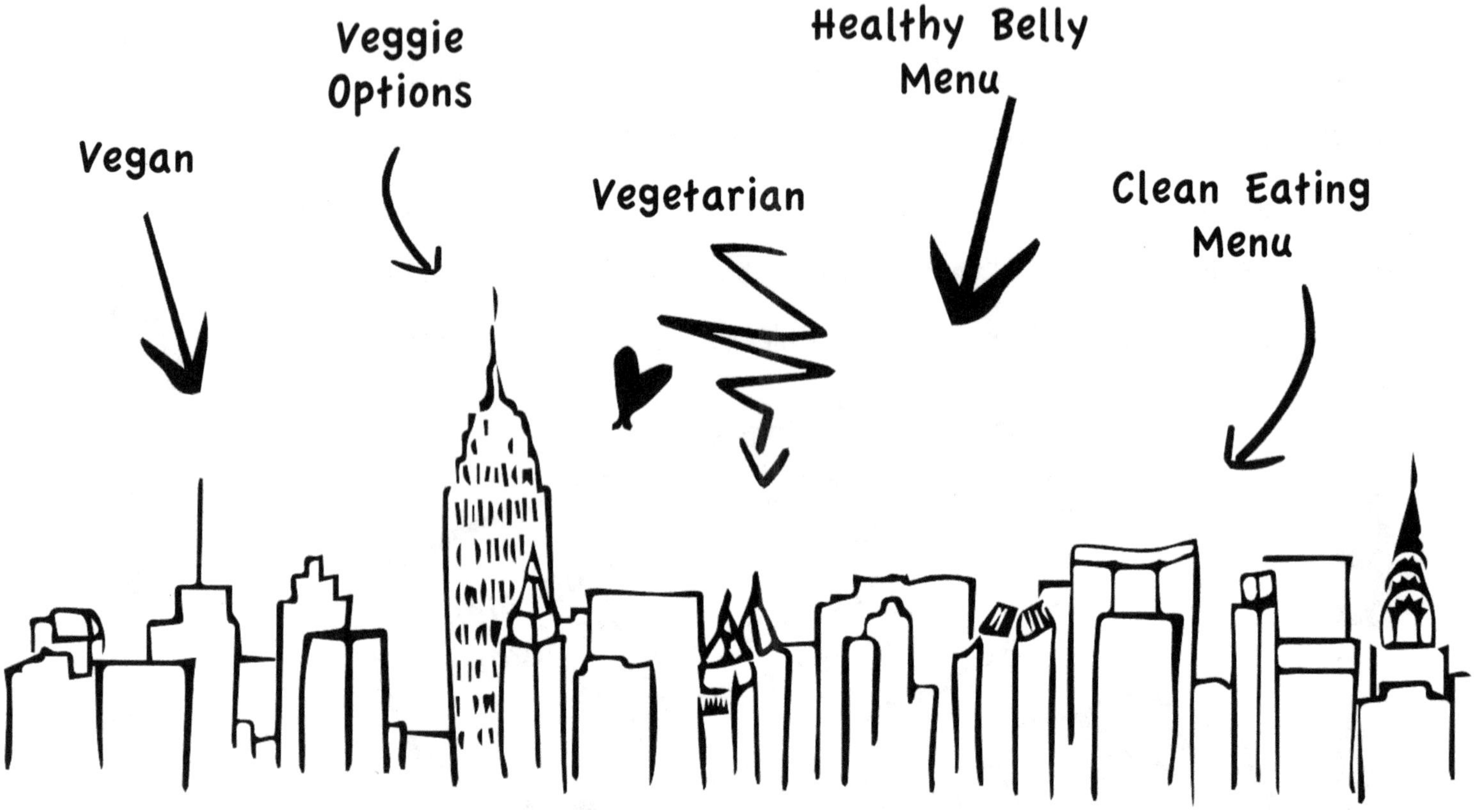

Vegan
Veggie Options
Vegetarian
Healthy Belly Menu
Clean Eating Menu

Today, everyone's talking about CLEAN EATING – and "everyone talking" means more resources are available to help you move toward a clean eating, HEALTHY lifestyle. But what exactly does clean eating mean?

For starters, you don't have to be a vegan to eat clean – or a vegetarian (a plant-based diet that includes dairy) for that matter. Your diet shifts to INCLUDE veggies and fruits, whole grains, more plant-based proteins, nuts, seeds, and oils. Think about it this way – you're consuming the good stuff that nature makes, not the factory.

POP QUIZ What have you **EATEN TODAY**?

Breakfast: ____________________

Lunch: ____________________

Snacks: ____________________

Dinner: ____________________

Snacks: ____________________

Beverages: ____________________

CLEAN EATING means kicking the processed and refined stuff to the curb. Yep, wave goodbye to the ~~sugary sodas and drinks~~, the ~~Twinkies and candy bars~~, the ~~potato chips and Hot Cheetos~~. Clean eating forces us to get our butts to the grocery store so we can cook our own food. This is the only way to truly know what's going into our bellies and straight to our brains.

HELP

What's a preservative anyway?
NO, REALLY...
someone email me about that
Erikakendrick@gmail.com

Another question I get is..."What should I buy at the store?"

START WITH YOUR...

VIP

HEALTHY BELLY LIST

What are your healthy faves?

Fruit: ______________________

____

____

Veggies: ______________________

____

____

Lean protein: ______________________

____

____

Snacks: ______________________

____

____

I'm a sucker for bananas, blueberries, and strawberries. And pineapples have always been at the top of my list. Recently, I've fallen in love with grapefruit; I put half of one in my daily Morning Magic Smoothies. On the veggie end, I'm always down for broccoli, cauliflower, and brussel sprouts. Add on bell peppers – all colors – and carrots, red onion, and spinach. I used to spit these healthies into my napkin and hide the napkin under the table when I was younger. The dog usually ratted me out. Now, they're my preferred babies. Sautéed. Raw. Grilled. Roasted. Yes, please!

THE SUPER SMART FOLKS AT HARVARD[3] SAY...

1. Make half your meal vegetables and fruits.
2. Choose whole grains whenever you can. Limit refined grains, like white rice and white bread, because the body rapidly turns them into blood sugar.
3. Pick the healthiest sources of protein, such as fish, poultry, beans, and nuts. Cut back on red meat; avoid bacon, cold cuts, & other processed meats.
4. Healthy oils (like olive and canola oil) are good for you.
5. Drink water, tea, or coffee. Milk and dairy are not must-have foods. Limit them to 1-2 servings a day, if at all.

Here's a look at a FOOD JOURNAL I kept for a few days. I totally get that it may not be the most exciting, but it gets my belly going and it's mostly clean eating. My brain isn't in pain and sizzly (yes, my brain sizzles from high fructose anything and numbered colorings - aka dyes - in food. And it shuts down from lard, hormones, steroids...) What can I say? I feel what I eat. And since I'm all about managing my moods, it starts with what I feed my brain.

MY HEALTHY BELLY FOOD JOURNAL

• I'm a vegan, so you might sub lean meat or low-fat dairy

MONDAY

Breakfast: Morning Magic Green Veggie Smoothie. Black Coffee

Snack: Whole Grain Oatmeal with blueberries and banana chunks

Lunch: Wrap-Star featuring The Mushrooms

Snack: Spicy Girl Kale Chips baked in my faithful oven

Dinner: Mushroom and Veggie Lettuce Cups with eggplant, broccoli, yellow bell peppers, black beans and brown rice. (from Big Veggie Haul thrown on the grill on Sunday)

TUESDAY

Breakfast: Sunshine Smoothie (with chia, flax, & vegan protein added). Black Coffee
Snack: Oatmeal with walnuts and strawberry slices
Lunch: Taco Tuesday's Mushroom and Veggie Tacos
Snack: Chips (don't judge me)
Dinner: Taco Tuesday Monster Salad (broccoli, bell pepper, mushrooms, cucumber, carrots, almond slivers, zucchini) and homemade dressing.

WEDNESDAY

Breakfast: Chocolate Swirl Smoothie with Cacao. Black Coffee
Snack: Oatmeal with banana chunks and blueberry bites
Lunch: Black Bean Burger smashed between lettuce cups. Leftover Salad
Snack: Coconut Brussel Chips – Brussel Sprout Chips slathered in coconut oil and baked in my faithful oven for 6-8 minutes. Chipotle salt.
Dinner: Brown Rice Bowl with my homemade Boss Sauce. Featuring broccoli, cauliflower, kale, brown rice, red bell peppers, mushrooms.

SMOOTHIE SPECIAL GUEST STARS:

gogi berries, chia seeds, hemp seeds, cacao powder, maca powder

Some of my other faves are my Power Girl Salad and my Queen-Wa Burrito with homemade Spicy Girl Sauce. I've also perfected my Pretty Little Pizzas made with tortilla crust. So much yum.

I love homemade, because, again... **PRESERVATIVES**! Seriously, email me about that!

Cheese Replacements

- ☐ Daiya
- ☐ Soya Kaas
- ☐ Sunergia Soyfoods
- ☐ Follow Your Heart and Galaxy Nutritional Foods are all good and come in cheddar, mozzarella, parmesan and feta

Dairy/Milk Replacements

- ☐ Rice, Almond, Oat or Soy milk

Other Non-Dairy Essentials

- ☐ Cream cheese and sour cream (Tofutti)
- ☐ Coffee creamer (Silk Soy Creamer)

Condiments

- ☐ Mayonnaise (Vegenaise mayonnaise)
- ☐ Ketchup, mustard, relish (Annie's Naturals, Cascadian Farm and Organicville are good)

Egg Substitute

- ☐ Ener-G Egg Replacer

Canned Goods

- ☐ Pasta sauces, beans and vegetables (try Eden Organic or Muir Glen)

Vegan Cooking Stocks and Broths

- ☐ Imagine Foods Organic No-Chicken Broth
- ☐ Imagine Foods Organic Vegetable Broth
- ☐ Pacific Natural Foods Organic Mushroom Broth
- ☐ Pacific Natural Foods Organic Vegetable Broth
- ☐ Rapunzel Vegetable Broth
- ☐ Better Than Bouillon No Beef Base
- ☐ Better Than Bouillon No Chicken Base

Frozen Foods/Meat Replacements

- ☐ Gardein frozen products (all vegan)
- ☐ Morningstar Farms Hickory BBQ Riblets
- ☐ Morningstar Farms Chick'n strips
- ☐ Nate's Meatless Meatballs
- ☐ Nate's Meatless Nuggets
- ☐ Amy's Bowl: Brown Rice, Black-Eyed Peas & Veggies
- ☐ Amy's Veggie Loaf (with mashed potatoes and veggies)
- ☐ Amy's Indian: Vegetable Korma or Mattar Tofu
- ☐ Amy's Enchilada or Burrito Especial
- ☐ Kashi Black Bean Mango
- ☐ Kashi Mayan Harvest Bake
- ☐ Kashi Tuscan Veggie Bake
- ☐ Amy's Bistro Burger (gluten-free)
- ☐ Sunshine Veggie Burgers
- ☐ Morningstar Farms Grillers (vegan)

Refrigerated Section

- ☐ Food for Life Sprouted Corn Tortillas
- ☐ Lightlife Smart Dogs
- ☐ Lightlife Organic Three Grain Tempeh
- ☐ Tofurky Italian Deli Slices
- ☐ Tofurky Italian Sausages
- ☐ WestSoy Baked Tofu, Italian-style
- ☐ Gardein products
- ☐ High-protein organic tofu and organic baked tofu
- ☐ Chicken-less Stuffed Cutlet
- ☐ Sweet potato spears
- ☐ Lentils, served hot or cold
- ☐ Hummus

Breakfast/Cereal

- ☐ Nature's Path Frozen Waffles (gluten-free, original and flax-plus)
- ☐ Amy's Mexican Tofu Scramble
- ☐ Natural Toasted Oat Bran
- ☐ Organic Oat & Flax
- ☐ Organic Cinnamon Spice Oatmeal
- ☐ Instant and regular organic steel-cut oats
- ☐ Kashi 7 Whole Grain Puffs
- ☐ Kashi Island Vanilla
- ☐ Kashi Strawberry Fields
- ☐ Kashi Autumn Wheat
- ☐ Kashi Heart to Heart Oat Flakes & Blueberry Clusters
- ☐ Kashi GOLEAN Crisp! Toasted Berry Crumble
- ☐ Kashi 7 Whole Grain Flakes
- ☐ Kashi Heart to Heart Oatmeal

Organic Grains/Breads

- ☐ Whole grains: brown or wild rice, millet, quinoa, amaranth, buckwheat, corn, etc.
- ☐ Flax crackers, rice cakes
- ☐ Steel-cut oats
- ☐ Whole grain breads (try the sprouted ones; go for gluten-free if you are sensitive to gluten)
- ☐ Whole grain pastas made from artichoke, wheat, corn, quinoa, spelt, black beans or rice
- ☐ Brown-rice pasta (fusilli, penne)

- ❑ Polenta
- ❑ Whole-wheat couscous
- ❑ Brown-rice bread

Kid's Favorites

- ❑ Health is Wealth Chicken-Free Vegan Nuggets and Patties
- ❑ Ian's Mac & No Cheese (wheat-free and gluten-free)
- ❑ Amy's Rice Mac & Cheese
- ❑ Thai Kitchen Noodle kits
- ❑ Tofutti Better Than Cream Cheese and Bagel
- ❑ Soy yogurt
- ❑ Cascadian Farm granola bars
- ❑ Crinkled wedge potatoes (frozen)
- ❑ Meatless corn dogs (frozen)
- ❑ Meatless meatballs (frozen)
- ❑ Bean & rice burritos
- ❑ Toaster waffles (frozen)
- ❑ Organic brown-rice pasta (fusilli, penne)

Vegetables and Fruits

- ❑ Avocados, squashes, broccoli, kale, mustard greens, Swiss chard, cucumbers, carrots, radishes, tomatoes, artichokes, cauliflower, Brussels sprout, eggplant, all kinds of mushrooms, salad greens, sweet potatoes (yams, roasting potatoes)
- ❑ Dried figs, apples, plums, blood oranges, cherries, blueberries, limes, etc.

Snack Ideas

- ❑ Dips and Garden Fresh Salsa
- ❑ Clif Bars
- ❑ Dried fruit
- ❑ Prepared hummus
- ❑ Baba ghanoush
- ❑ Cascadian Farm granola bars
- ❑ Sweet potato breakfast pudding
- ❑ Root vegetable corn chips
- ❑ Popcorn
- ❑ Corn chip dippers
- ❑ Nut butters (almond, peanut, sunflower seed)
- ❑ Trail mixes
- ❑ Nuts
- ❑ Organic brown rice cakes
- ❑ Kettle corn
- ❑ Salt & Pepper Crisps
- ❑ Flax crackers
- ❑ Wasa crackers with nut butter and agave

Desserts/Non-Dairy Ice Cream

- ❑ Purely Decadent
- ❑ It's Soy Delicious
- ❑ Rice Dream
- ❑ Luna & Larry's Organic Coconut Bliss
- ❑ Living Harvest Tempt Hemp Milk
- ❑ Good Karma, Organic Rice Divine
- ❑ Tofutti
- ❑ Tofutti Cuties (ice cream sandwiches)
- ❑ Sorbets
- ❑ 72% dark or bittersweet chocolate (any chocolate marked over 70% is non-dairy, and now you can even find "milk" chocolate made from rice milk)
- ❑ Vegan cookies
- ❑ Soy Dream soy creams
- ❑ Vegan chocolate mousse

DID YOU KNOW...

Research linking diet and mental health shows that food—along with other factors—plays an important contributing role in the development, management and prevention of specific mental health problems such as depression, schizophrenia, attention deficit hyperactivity disorder (ADHD) and Alzheimer's disease.[5]

Enjoy designing your **HEALTHY BELLY MENU** for the week. Remember to include all the yummy stuff you love. *After each day, reflect.*

SUNDAY

Breakfast

Snack

Lunch

Snack

Dinner

Reflection

MONDAY

Breakfast

Snack

Lunch

Snack

Dinner

Reflection

TUESDAY

Breakfast

Snack

Lunch

Snack

Dinner

Reflection

WEDNESDAY

Breakfast

Snack

Lunch

Snack

Dinner

Reflection

THURSDAY

Breakfast

Snack

Lunch

Snack

Dinner

Reflection

FRIDAY

Breakfast

Snack

Lunch

Snack

Dinner

Reflection

SATURDAY

Breakfast

Snack

Lunch

Snack

Dinner

Reflection

A quick stroll through the bookstore turns up an array of clean eating cookbooks and THE Google always introduces some new and exciting recipes. And if you're still stuck, check out:

Ms. Skinny's grocery list: (http://skinnyms.com/the-ultimate-clean-eating-grocery-list-50-foods/)

Cooking Light also outlines recipes for you to enjoy for each meal, including options for eating out: (http://www.cookinglight.com/eating-smart/smart-choices/clean-eating-guide)

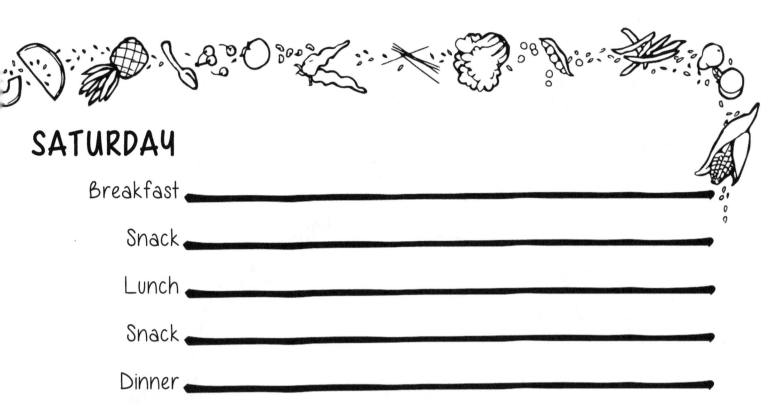

color me

Four

VISUALIZING YOUR HAPPY

Where's your happy place?

You know, the place that makes you feel warm and fuzzy, happy and joyful, content and serene when you think about it? Where's yours?

My happy place is ______________________________

____

____

____

Visualizing is a cool form of meditation that involves using all your senses to magically transport you to your happy place. It's a sensory relaxation experience that asks how does that place feel, smell, look, taste, and sound? When I visualize my happy place, I'm instantly transported to a gorgeous beach in Malibu, overlooking the Pacific Ocean. I heart the 'Bu.

YOUR HAPPY PLACE

When I close my eyes, I see

I hear

I can smell

I can taste

I can feel the

At my happy place, I see myself ____________________

When I'm at my happy place, I feel ____________________

Science has shown that the subconscious mind is unable to distinguish between a vivid visualization and an actual real-life experience.[6]

9 OUT OF 10 PEOPLE told me their HAPPY PLACE was somewhere near a body of water or a beach. *Those are my people!*

My happy place

When I close my eyes, I see myself on a beautiful beach in Bali or on the oversized deck of a sweet cottage in Summerland overlooking the Pacific Ocean. But my all time fave is still Malibu. I take a few deep, cleansing breaths, relax my body, and I'm surrounded by MY HAPPY.

I SEE myself walking in the warm sand. I HEAR AND FEEL the water rippling around my feet. The air, heated by the golden sun against my shoulders, wraps me in a familiar hug. I TASTE the salty air and SMELL the coconut-infused tanning lotion against my skin. The palm trees dance in the breeze, greeting me, as I lose myself in my happy.

DRAW OR PASTE A PICTURE OF YOUR HAPPY PLACE

CKET
01234
01234
TICKET
TO ENTER HAPPY PLACE
01234
01234
TICK

INSTRUCTIONS FOR TRANSPORT

1. **GET COMFY.** Sitting is always good for me so I don't fall asleep.
2. **IDENTIFY YOUR HAPPY PLACE** (beach, cabin in the woods, rainforest, top of Mt. Everest, you get the point).
3. **RELAX YOUR BODY.** *Progressive Muscle Relaxation* is my jam! I do this whenever and wherever I need to take five and relax.

SECRETS TO PROGRESSIVE MUSCLE RELAXATION

- ✓ Close your eyes.
- ✓ Tense your toes on one foot.
- ✓ Hold it for 5 seconds and relax.
- ✓ Do the same thing on the other foot.
- ✓ Then move up the whole body.

4. **START VISUALIZING** by experiencing your happy place with all five of your senses. Try your best to experience every detail of your happy place in your mind. See yourself there. Feel yourself there. What do you see? How does it smell? What do you feel? What do you hear? How does it taste?

Make a collage of your happy place

VISIT YOUR HAPPY PLACE

Cut out magazine pictures and words that describe your HAPPY PLACE and paste them on your page.

AT LEAST ONCE A DAY

Five

MEDITATION

Sometimes dating can change your life for the better. Sometimes. When I stumbled into meditation, it was because of a guy I was dating. I don't remember his name, but I'll always be in gratitude for the gift he gave me - my absolute favorite book, *Way of the Peaceful Warrior*. After reading it, my mindset shifted; it was like someone turned on the light bulbs in my brain. Sound cooky? A little on the granola side? Well, that's exactly what I thought until I realized the benefits of sitting in stillness and being aware of my thoughts - but without attachment. The peaceful calm that came from meditating was one of the most radical things I'd ever experienced.

Many experts believe that Mindful Meditation helps with depression, substance abuse, eating disorders, anxiety, obsessive-compulsive disorder, and sleep disorder.[7]

color me

Practicing Mindfulness can help you gain control over your thoughts and free you from your Stinkin' Thinkin'.

My first attempt at meditating was A BIG DUD! I couldn't sit still for longer than five minutes, and if I'm being generous, maybe I was able to be attentive to my thoughts for two of those five minutes. After minute two, my highly advanced stinkin' thinkin' hijacked my mind and led me down a dark, windy road toward blame, shame, and guilt. But something kept calling me back to the practice, and luckily, I listened.

Lesson: Be patient with yourself!

PREP TO MEDITATE

FIND A QUIET SPACE

GRAB A TIMER

Your cell phone works perfectly!

SET YOUR TIMER for 5 minutes.

But the big goal is to practice stillness for at least twenty minutes.

Namaste

If you're new to meditating, try not to feel overwhelmed or anxious. That defeats the entire purpose. To put it simply, no matter what brand of meditation you're adopting, the primary focus of the practice is:

POSTURE
BREATHING
ATTENTION TO YOUR THOUGHTS
RELAXATION

And if you'd rather not just plop yourself on the floor, sit cross-legged on your tushie, and breathe mindfully. There are cool resources and tools out there to help you ease into your mindfulness journey.

For guided meditation for beginners,

check out iTunes, Spotify, YouTube...
or a quick Google search will pull up tons on the practice, too.

5 STEPS to Meditating

1. **GET COMFORTABLE** in a quiet space.

2. **GET IN POSITION.** Sit cross-legged on the floor or in a chair. You might want a soft cushion under your tush. I sit on a shaggy rug.

3. **RELAX.** Close your eyes and begin taking deep breaths. Breathe in deeply from your abdomen and out through your nose or mouth.

4. **FOCUS ON YOUR BREATH.** Slowly inhale positive energy, slowly exhale negativity.

5. **DO NOT TRY AND STOP YOUR THOUGHTS** or empty your mind. Whenever you become aware that your attention has drifted back to your thoughts or any other distractions, focus on your breathing again.

Now when I meditate, I sit in silence for a minimum of twenty minutes and go deep inside of, well, me. And when the thoughts try to race through my mind – because they ALWAYS do - I gently and lovingly dismiss them with a deliberate breath.

TODAY, my moods are more stabilized and I'm super aware of the thoughts that move through my mind, even the stinkin' thinkin' ones. Remember to take small steps toward achieving your goals and, most importantly, be gentle with yourself.

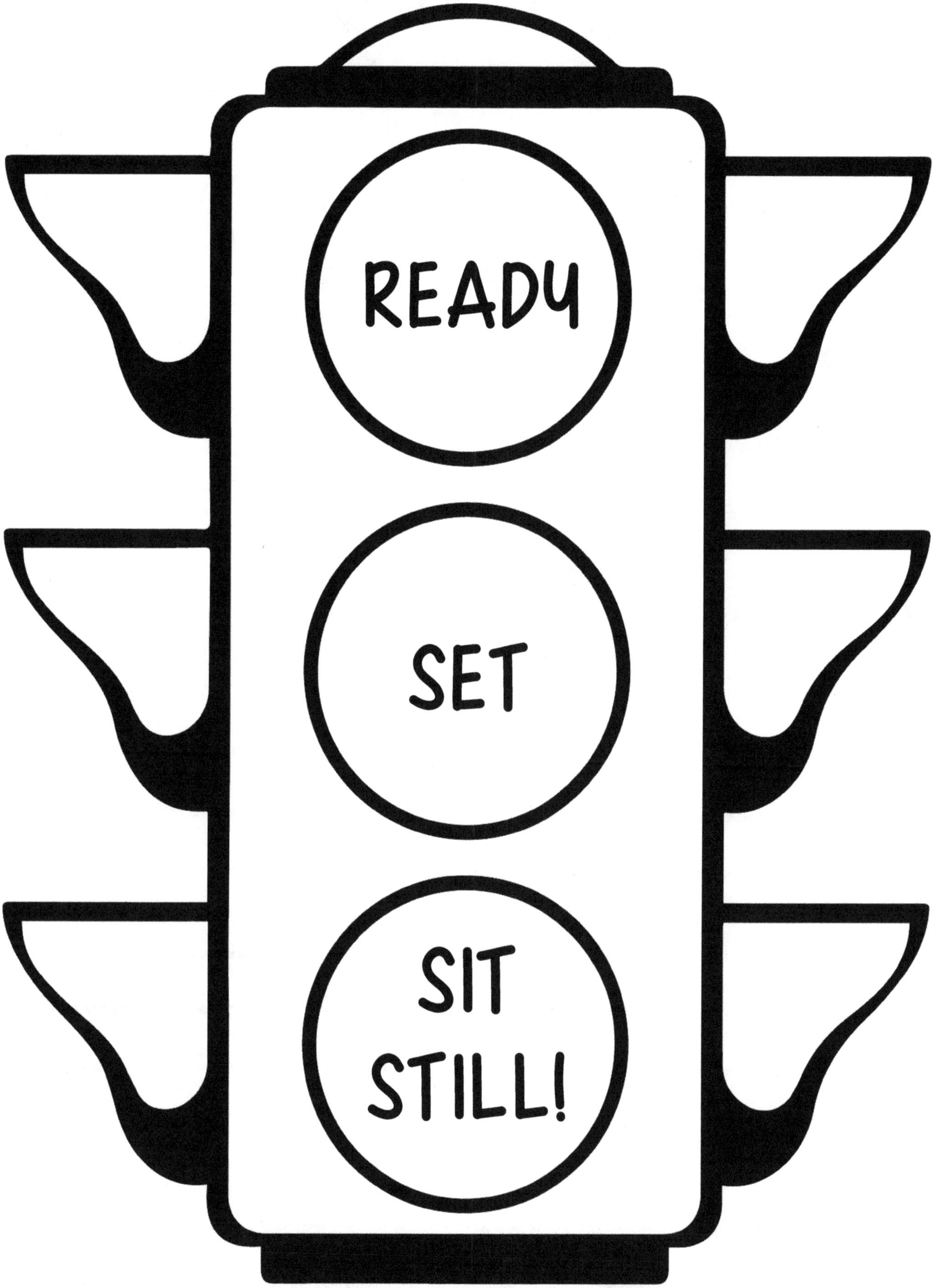
READY
SET
SIT
STILL!

Congratulations! **YOU DID IT!**

How was your experience Namaste-ing?

How positive was your experience?	1	2	3	4	5
How challenging was it to practice stillness?	1	2	3	4	5
How positive were your thoughts?	1	2	3	4	5
How intense was your stinkin' thinkin'?	1	2	3	4	5
How successful were you in detaching from your thoughts?	1	2	3	4	5

My OVERALL EXPERIENCE meditating was

The most challenging part was

I found myself getting distracted with thoughts about

When thoughts would arise, I

I was able to sit in stillness for minutes.

Next time, in order to have a better experience, I'm going to

Right now, I'm feeling

Ready Set **GOALS**

I'm going to meditate ________ days out of the week.

I'm going to dedicate ________ minutes to practicing meditation.

BOOK YOURSELF

	SUN	MON	TUE	WED	THU	FRI	SAT
WEEK 1							
WEEK 2							
WEEK 3							
WEEK 4							

FLESH OUT YOUR MEDITATION SCHEDULE!

Save time to REFLECT after each session.

SUNDAY

Time: ____________

Location: ____________

I successfully meditated for ________ minutes today.

I felt more calm and relaxed after I was done. **YES NO**

I was able to sit in stillness and detach from my thoughts. **YES NO**

I was distracted by ____________

Goals: The next time I mediate, I'm going to be sure to

____

____

____

MONDAY

Time: ____________________

Location: ____

I successfully meditated for ________ minutes today.

I felt more calm and relaxed after I was done. **YES NO**

I was able to sit in stillness and detach from my thoughts. **YES NO**

I was distracted by ________________________________

Goals: The next time I mediate, I'm going to be sure to

____

____

____

TUESDAY

Time: ____________________

Location: ____

I successfully meditated for ________ minutes today.

I felt more calm and relaxed after I was done. **YES NO**

I was able to sit in stillness and detach from my thoughts. **YES NO**

I was distracted by ________________________________

Goals: The next time I mediate, I'm going to be sure to

____

____

____

WEDNESDAY

Time: ______________

Location: ______________________________

I successfully meditated for ________ minutes today.

I felt more calm and relaxed after I was done. **YES** **NO**

I was able to sit in stillness and detach from my thoughts. **YES** **NO**

I was distracted by ______________________________

Goals: The next time I mediate, I'm going to be sure to

____

____

____

THURSDAY

Time: ______________

Location: ______________________________

I successfully meditated for ________ minutes today.

I felt more calm and relaxed after I was done. **YES** **NO**

I was able to sit in stillness and detach from my thoughts. **YES** **NO**

I was distracted by ______________________________

Goals: The next time I mediate, I'm going to be sure to

____

____

____

FRIDAY

Time: ______________

Location: ______________________________

I successfully meditated for ________ minutes today.

I felt more calm and relaxed after I was done. **YES** **NO**

I was able to sit in stillness and detach from my thoughts. **YES** **NO**

I was distracted by ______________________________

Goals: The next time I mediate, I'm going to be sure to

____

____

____

SATURDAY

Time: ______________

Location: ______________________________

I successfully meditated for ________ minutes today.

I felt more calm and relaxed after I was done. **YES** **NO**

I was able to sit in stillness and detach from my thoughts. **YES** **NO**

I was distracted by ______________________________

Goals: The next time I mediate, I'm going to be sure to

____

____

____

Six

EXERCISE

When I'm feeling FRAGILE or BLAH AND BLUE, it's incredibly hard for me to exercise or to even think about being active. That's when I prefer to stay in bed and watch television – and I may or may not have a pint of vegan Ben & Jerry's Peanut Butter & Cookies ice cream under the covers with me.

Sometimes I'm so deep in my head-space that the television is actually watching me. But that's when I know I need to exercise more than anything. And I have to be super deliberate about it.

MY CHEAT SHEET

I need...

1

AN AMAZING WORKOUT PLAYLIST.

Music that's going to MAKE ME want to move!

2

TO SEE MY WORKOUT GEAR.

I'm not really into cutesy outfits so all I need to see are my sneakers and my running pants. But if a cute outfit does it for you, toss it over your bed so you can see it.

3

TO RUN OUT THE DOOR.

Fast!

Did you know . . . ?

A clinical psychologist at Duke University named James Blumenthal discovered that antidepressants and exercise had the same effects on patients suffering from major depression.[8]

YOUR TOP 10 WAYS YOU LIKE TO STAY ACTIVE...

1. ______________________________

2. ______________________________

3. ______________________________

4. ______________________________

5. ______________________________

6. ______________________________

7. ______________________________

8. ______________________________

9. ______________________________

10. ______________________________

When you just don't feel like hitting the gym, go to your list of activities that *don't include* a treadmill or a single weight.

Here are some more "nope, not the gym" ways to stay active!

WALKING

JOGGING

SWIMMING

HIKING

SKATING

BIKING

CANOEING

ZUMBA

TENNIS

DANCING (...HIP HOP, SALSA, FOLK, LINE, JAZZ...)

KICK BOXING

CLEANING

FRISBEE

There are tremendous benefits to exercise. The feel good chemicals, endorphins and serotonin, are released in the brain and improve your mood. Exercise reduces loneliness, stress, depression and anxiety, and improves sleep.[9] And who doesn't want all of that in their lives? Me!

More tricks to get the

ENDORPHINS FLOWING!

1. Take the STAIRS instead of the elevator.
2. WALK or RIDE your bike to work, school, or to run errands.
3. PARK in the back of the lot at the grocery store or work.

Ready Set GOALS

If you're not already dedicated to a workout/exercise schedule, then now is the perfect time to build one. Start small and work your way up to your big goals.

MY BIG GOAL was to run three miles at least three times a week. I started with walking by the ocean. Over time, I was able to jalk (jog/walk – yep, I made up that word). Then I was able to build up to a jog for most of the route. Now, I jog as part of my warm up and then I run the rest of the way. It took months to accomplish my goal, but I kept at it. And you can too.

Keep track of your goals and your progress...
You'll see your improvement over time.

My favorite part is rewarding myself with a new thrift shop find. But then, I guess that isn't new, is it... more like used. But you get the point. So get your rewards ready!

BOOK YOURSELF

Sometimes it's even better with a friend

AT LEAST 30 MINUTES OF EXERCISE A DAY!

	Goal Time	Activity	Support Squad	Results
SUN	*2-3pm*	*Bike ride*	*Jennifer*	*One hour on bike; EXCITED about tomorrow*
MON				
TUE				
WED				
THU				
FRI				
SAT				

Post workout week
ASSESSMENT

After challenging yourself with your workout goals, how do you feel?

I was able to accomplish my workout goals because I...

I was not able to accomplish my workout goals. Some of my obstacles were...

Next time, I will make sure that I...

I make sure to avoid...

I'm concerned about...

I'm looking forward to...

Overall, I feel...

SELFIE TIME!

YOU & your FAVE activity...

Seven

SLEEP zzZZZ

SLEEP is the real MVP! Catching z's is one of my all-time favorite activities. And after a good eight hours, I wake up feeling like a rockstar. But if I go too many days without a good night's rest, I might as well be hallucinating. Seriously. Each blink feels like my eyelids are lifting weights, my thoughts are muddied, and my concentration goes on strike. Not to be outdone, my anxiety shoots through the roof with my paranoia riding shotgun. RESTful sleep is a CRITICAL part of my Mental Fitness Plan. Without it, I'm a mental breakdown waiting to happen.

The Harvard Medical Review smarties suggest that a good night's sleep helps foster both mental and emotional resilience, while chronic sleep disruptions set the stage for negative thinking and emotional vulnerability.[10]

color me

It took me years to finally accept that my body needs to reboot; running on fumes does not work for me. I learned that lesson after cramming and pulling all-nighters for papers and presentations. FACT: My stinkin' thinkin' and my brain pain are sometimes linked to my sleep issues.

HARVARD SMARTIES SAY[11]...

1. **SLEEP PROBLEMS** are more likely to affect patients with psychiatric disorders than people in the general population.

2. **SLEEP PROBLEMS** may increase risk for developing particular mental illnesses, as well as result from such disorders.

3. **TREATING** the sleep disorder may help alleviate symptoms of the mental health problem.

MY SLEEP ASSESSMENT

CIRCLE A HAPPY OR ANGRY SLEEPER.

YES NO

I play or work on my phone before bed.

I drink alcohol before bed.

I drink caffeinated drinks before bed.

I sleep in a bedroom with a good temperature.

I eat less than three hours before bedtime.

I exercise regularly.

I have a calming bedtime routine.

I take naps during the day.

I watch TV in bed.

I sleep with blackout curtains.

I do relaxing exercises before bed.

I sleep with a mask covering my eyes.

HOW MANY HAPPY SLEEPERS DID YOU COLLECT?

MY SLEEP JOURNAL

The Bedtime Breakdown

	# of times I woke up	# of caffeinated drinks yesterday	# of alcoholic drinks yesterday	Time I went to sleep	Time I woke up	# of hours slept	This Morning I felt... (1-5)
SUN							
MON							
TUE							
WED							
THU							
FRI							
SAT							

BEDTIME REFLECTION JOURNAL:

Complete your Sleep Journal at least one hour before bed.

Sunday

Today was a ______________ day. Right now, I'm feeling...

To get ready for bed, for the next hour, I'm going to...

Monday

Today was a ______________ day. Right now, I'm feeling...

To get ready for bed, for the next hour, I'm going to...

Tuesday

Today was a ________________ day. Right now, I'm feeling...

To get ready for bed, for the next hour, I'm going to...

Wednesday

Today was a ________________ day. Right now, I'm feeling...

To get ready for bed, for the next hour, I'm going to...

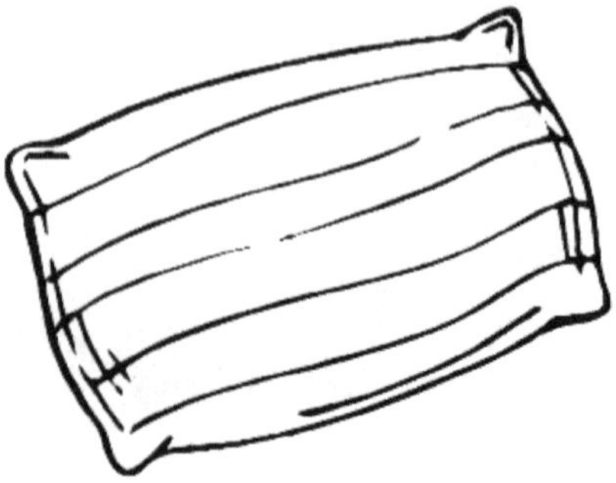

Sleep

Thursday

Today was a ________________ day. Right now, I'm feeling...

To get ready for bed, for the next hour, I'm going to...

Friday

Today was a ________________ day. Right now, I'm feeling...

To get ready for bed, for the next hour, I'm going to...

Book

SLEEP

Saturday

Today was a ______________________ day. Right now, I'm feeling...

____

____

____

To get ready for bed, for the next hour, I'm going to...

____

____

____

- Fitbit & activity monitors are amazing sleep trackers.

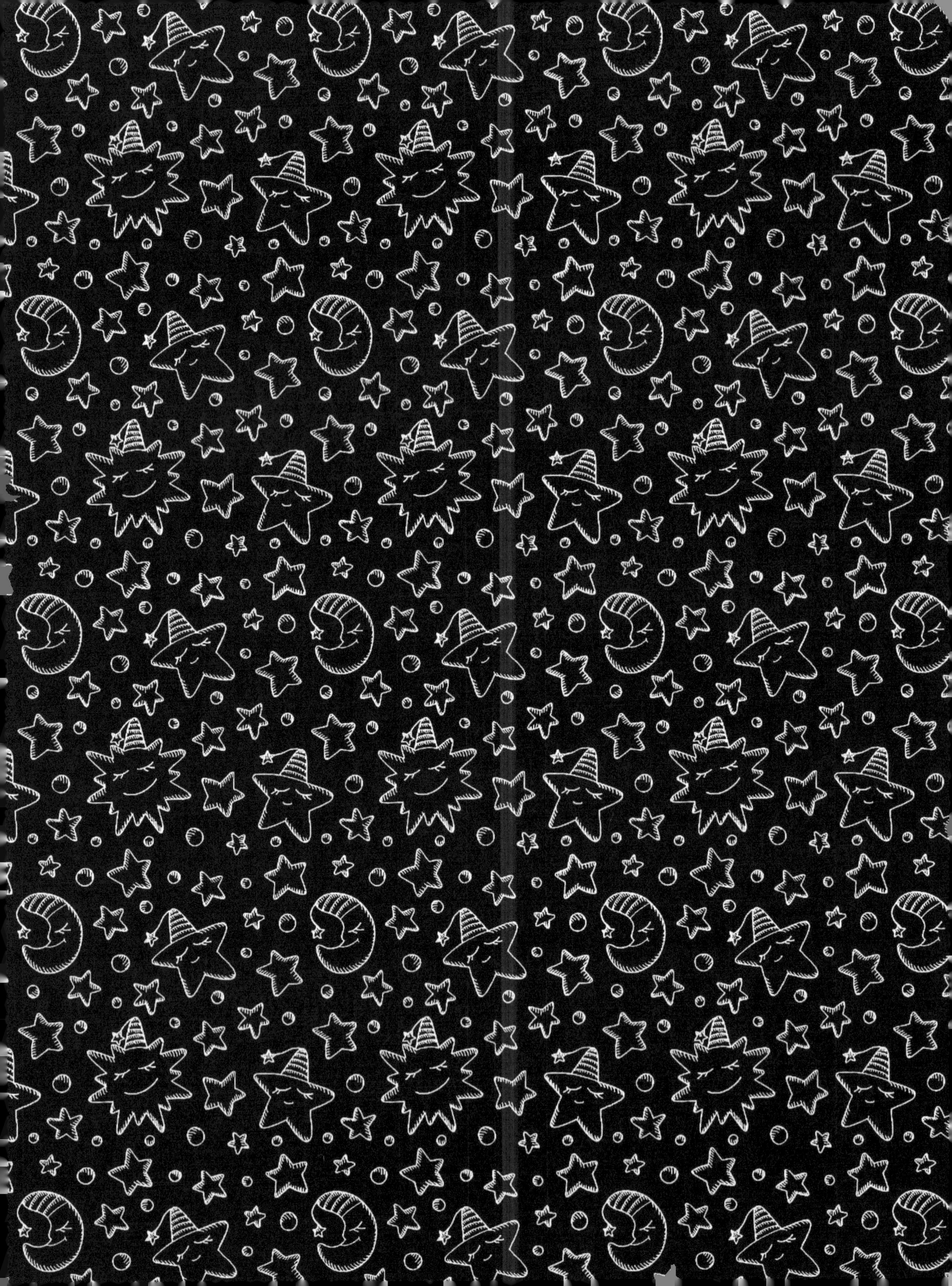

Eight

MP3

MUSIC is...

My jam

My lifeline

My nirvana

My ecstasy

My air

My breath

My love

My savior

My escape

My soundtrack

My world

My everything

My vibration

My frequency

My elevation

My peace

My church

My heartbeat

My soul

My joy

My blessing

My energy

My spirit

My passion

My comfort

My indulgence

My truth

My cool

My walk

My swag

My happy

I love music and I can often be found with my earbuds stuck in my ears with one of my playlists blasting. Music not only helps keep me in a groovy mood space, it also serves to ward off negative energy around me. I've learned that I'm very receptive to energy (most of us creatives are) and music serves as a blocker, especially when I'm not centered or when I'm feeling particularly fragile. I've learned how to recognize my triggers and my music is often my armor. Have you ever really thought about your relationship with music?

Did you know?

Music affects the levels of oxytocin in the brain… it evokes feelings of contentment, reductions in anxiety, and feelings of calmness and security.[12]

Let's have a look . . .

I ♥ MUSIC

MY MUSIC MENTALITY

I listen to music ________ times a day.

I listen to music ________ hours each day.

Music makes me feel:

____

____

____

I like to listen to music when:

____

____

____

My all time
FAVORITE SONG

Song: ______________________

By: ______________________

When I listen to my FAVORITE song, I feel...

____

____

The last time I listened to my favorite song was...

____

____

The last time I listened to my favorite song, I was...

____

____

When I listen to my favorite song, it makes me want to...

____

____

Lyrics to my **FAV**

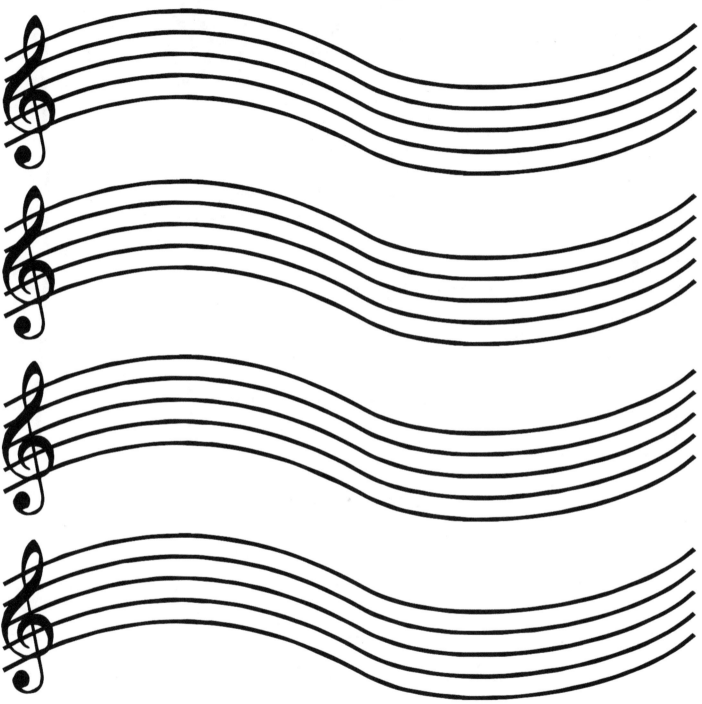

I have eclectic taste and I rock out to everything from John Mayer and Drake to Beyoncé and Banks. The good energy mix from the base and treble center my vibration. Music feeds my soul and elevates my HAPPY. It's EMPOWERING to be in control of that, especially with moods that get off on seesawing back and forth.

MY HAPPY PLAYLISTS

My DJ Name is:

MY TOP 5

Any genre. Any artist. (Bonus if one is by Prince!)

Song	How does it make you feel?
1. ____________	____________
2. ____________	____________
3. ____________	____________
4. ____________	____________
5. ____________	____________

My playlists are as sacred to me as my phone, and that's pretty sacred. I have one playlist for working out, one for lounging around, one for writing, one for lazy beach days, one for shopping, one for driving the coast, one for cleaning, one for... you get the point. But I'm always careful not to listen to too many sappy, melancholy songs in a row. I love creating soundtracks to my life, and I love EVEN MORE that my music reduces stress and eases my anxiety. NAMASTE!

CREATE
Your Happy Soundtrack

	Song	Artist
1.		
2.		
3.		
4.		
5.		
6.		
7.		
8.		
9.		
10.		

When you're feeling DOWN, DEPRESSED, OR BLAH & BLUE, what 3 songs do you usually play? How do they make you feel?

Song	How does it make you feel?
1. ________	________
2. ________	________
3. ________	________

Would they make you more depressed? Would they pull you deeper into a dark hole?

BE CAREFUL NOT TO fuel your sadness when you're already feeling fragile. It's common to want to hear music that reflects your feelings, but don't overdo it. Always go back to your happy playlist! I STEER CLEAR OF ADELE! Just sayin'.

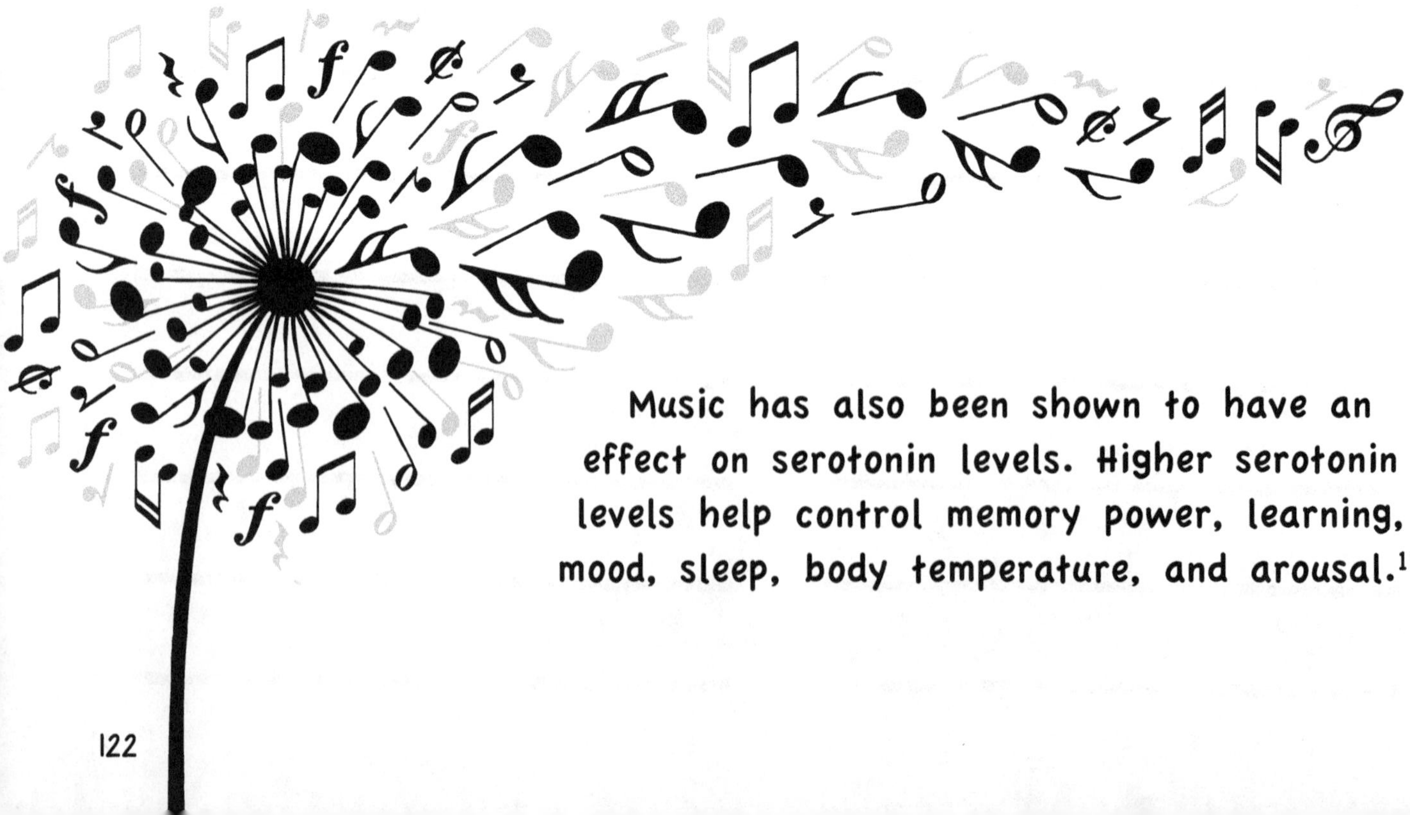

Music has also been shown to have an effect on serotonin levels. Higher serotonin levels help control memory power, learning, mood, sleep, body temperature, and arousal.[13]

DJ ______________________ 's Chill-Out Playlist

1. ______________________
2. ______________________
3. ______________________
4. ______________________
5. ______________________

DJ ______________________ 's I'm Feelin Myself Playlist

1. ______________________
2. ______________________
3. ______________________
4. ______________________
5. ______________________

DJ ______________________ 's Sweat It Out /Workout Playlist

1. ______________________
2. ______________________
3. ______________________
4. ______________________
5. ______________________

Nine

SOUL SERVICE

A professor of Preventative Medicine at Stony Brook University, says a part of our brain lights up when we help others. That part of our brain then doles out feel-good chemicals like dopamine, and possibly serotonin... they help us feel joy and delight – a real "helper's high".[14]

Most of my life, I've participated in some kind of long-term community service activity or joined organizations that valued service and prioritized it in their mission statement. My mom signed me up for Girl Scouts as a Brownie. I stayed all the way through high school. I even wore that green uniform to school as a senior whenever we had a Girl Scout activity planned. (My classmates respected the green sash!) Later, I joined a sorority that emphasized service, and I volunteered for an entertainment organization that helped industry professionals. No matter how old I was, or at what developmental stage, I always felt better after a good round of what I call Soul Service.

I enjoy being of service because it gives me time to think about making someone else's life experience better. Plus I get to forget about myself for a while. Good Soul Service also elevates my mood-i-tude and takes me to a place of gratitude, while connecting me to those I'm working with who share similar interests and values.

Your Top 5

Service Activities You Enjoy

EX. *Working with the homeless* ____________________

1. ____
2. ____
3. ____
4. ____
5. ____

Being of Soul Service can be done in many different ways and volunteering is at the top of that list. It's a great way to boost oxytocin – that feel good hormone that flushes through your system and floods it with warm fuzzies. Well, let's just say that oxytocin is my jam. Service always makes me feel good and can be just the boost I need when I'm slipping into a mild depression.

There are many ways to be of service - helping animals, working with people in hospitals, or servicing the elderly. As humans, we're supposed to connect with others, and being of soul service is, well, good for the soul.

Did you know?

Sara Konrath, a PhD and director of Interdisciplinary Program for Empathy and Altruism Research at the Univeristy of Michigan says that we are hard-wired for face-to-face contact that includes lots of touch, eye contact, and smiles. This releases oxytocin, which helps us bond and care for others, and also helps us handle stress better.[15]

Let's research

YOUR TOP 5

SOUL SERVICE OPTIONS

Activity	Website	Phone Number	Address	Hours to Commit	Notes
Homeless Shelter for teens	*homelessshelter.com*	*777-777-7777*	*1234 S. Walnut*	*2-4pm*	*Volunteers needed Mon & Wed to prepare meals. Apply online.*
1.					
2.					
3.					
4.					
5.					

Consider how many hours you will volunteer and which day(s) of the week you will commit to being of service.

Then it's time to *Sign on the dotted line*

Now, because we can get distracted by life, and also because we don't actually have to answer to anyone when we commit to participating in a service activity, it can be hard to pull ourselves together and actually show up on our committed day. Multiply this truth by 1,000,000,000,000,000 (that's like, a zillion!) when we're feeling blah and blue, and you have a recipe for an incomplete Soul Service Activity.

Complete your Soul Service Contract and remember that it's binding.

That means you are making a commitment to show up on time to be of Soul Service.

And then the best part...

REWARD YOURSELF

As an extra incentive...

PLAN YOUR REWARD(S) for completing your Soul Service.

SPA DAY
TAKE A NAP
ICE CREAM
MANI PEDI
SHOPPING
MAKEOVER
MOVIE DAY
CONCERT NIGHT
BUBBLE BATH
VIDEO GAME
WALK IN THE PARK
DATE NIGHT
BUY A GOOD BOOK
SALON VISIT
DANCE PARTY
NEW SHOES

♥ SOUL SERVICE CONTRACT ♥

My Name: ______________________________

Person you'll be helping or Soul Service Organization:

____

Describe the Soul Service work you'll be doing. (Be specific):

____

First and Last Name of Supervisor (Person who will supervise/direct you):

____

Person or Organization Telephone No.:

____

Person who will provide transportation (If you are not driving yourself):

____

Sign below.

I agree to the Soul Service Contract. I will arrive at ________(time) and I will be leave at ________(time).

Signature: ______________________________

Date: ______________________________

Pre-Date **JITTERS?**

BEFORE Your First Soul Service Date!

Going somewhere new and meeting new people can be a daunting task. If you're feeling anxiety as your service date approaches, *just know that I always do too.* In fact, many people get a case of the nerves when they are ADVENTURING into the unknown.

Your Anxiety Cheat Sheet:

Dance it out.

Turn up your Happy Playlist and dance it out.

Sleep it out.

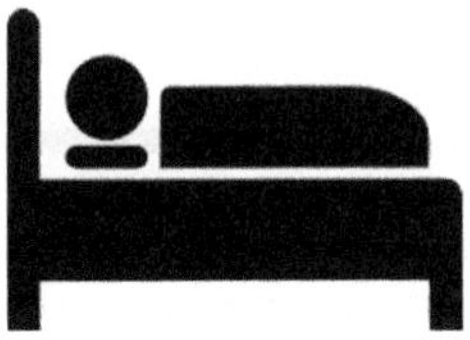

A good night's sleep always helps. Limit your alcohol and caffeine so you can have a smooth transition to *zzzzzzzzzz*.

Work it out.

Lace those sneakers, grab the water bottle, and get into a good workout.

Breathe it out.

Take ten deep breaths. Then take ten more. Slowly. Count to ten while you do it.

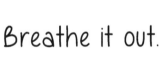

Vision it out.

Close your eyes and see yourself having a great Soul Service Activity. See yourself meeting new people and enjoying your time connecting with them.

Talk it out!

Reach out to someone on your Support Squad and share your feelings. They earned that spot on your VIP Squad, so call on them. You deserve it!

Post-Date Soul Service Reflection

I really enjoyed doing

I didn't like

Meeting was really cool. I liked the way he/she

At my next Soul Service Session, I'm going to be sure to

because

Before I went to volunteer, I was concerned about

but now that I've gone, I feel

Reflect and journal anything else you're feeling about your experience.

Was this a good Soul Service match for you? If it wasn't, double back to your TOP FIVE and call the next service activity you listed and repeat the process. Finding the right Soul Service match is just as important as being of service. And once you've found your Soul Service match, it's time to get you booked! I always love having calendar dates filled in and in front of me. That way I never forget the details, like showing up – and being on time.

Take a few minutes and complete your

Soul Service Calendar

Be sure to add anything you may need to remember, like bringing a hat or wearing sunscreen.

WEEK 1	Sunday	Monday	Tuesday	Wednesday	Thursday	Friday	Saturday
WEEK 2	Sunday	Monday	Tuesday	Wednesday	Thursday	Friday	Saturday
WEEK 3	Sunday	Monday	Tuesday	Wednesday	Thursday	Friday	Saturday
WEEK 4	Sunday	Monday	Tuesday	Wednesday	Thursday	Friday	Saturday

Awesome job! You should be very proud of yourself! Being of service to others is one of the kindest things you can do. Allow yourself the emotional space to smile at a job well done!

Ten

FURRY FRIENDS

I was a sophomore in college when I was diagnosed with severe acute depression. I'd spent my freshman year and half of my sophomore year far away from my cats; it was the first time I was away from my pets for an extended amount of time and it had definitely taken a toll on me. I'd had pets since I was a little girl and I recognized the void from not having a furry friend to love. As soon as I returned to Stanford the following year, I leased an off-campus studio apartment and marched right over to the animal shelter and found Tabitha, my new wild child.

That feisty feline made my apartment and my life feel settled, even though she tore up everything her little paws could find. But caring for her comforted me. Every day she fought me as I tried to domesticate her. I tried to put her in my purse and take her everywhere with me (including class) until she finally had enough and ran away. But somehow I understood her; the world was her oyster, one much bigger than my studio apartment in East Palo Alto.

NAME OF YOUR FAVORITE PET

HELLO
my name is

My favorite memory with my furry friend is

Studies have shown that being around pets is associated with lower blood pressure and heart rate, and fewer symptoms of anxiety and depression.[16]

My favorite thing to do with my furry friend is/was...

My furry friend always made/makes me feel...

Understood	Strong	Relaxed
Challenged Calm	Confident	Proud
Valued	Hopeful	Ready
Happy	Assured	Focused
Respected	Confident	
Powerful	Strong	

When I graduated from college and moved back to Chicago, my cousin gifted me with the most adorable kitten. I named him Cody. Over the next twenty years, that kitten grew to be my everything. I wouldn't leave home without him,

and unlike Tabitha, he didn't want to be left behind. Cody traveled everywhere with me and even accompanied me through some of my most haunting life challenges. I was diagnosed with bipolar disorder shortly after Cody came into my life. And I spent the next fifteen years trying to find purpose and meaning in the minutia of my every day, even after moving us to New York City.

On many of those days, Cody was both my meaning and my purpose. He comforted me when I was anxious or manic and soothed me during bouts of deep depression. When I contemplated suicide, he was always there to refocus my energy on the present and give those moments meaning.

By focusing on the animal and its needs, the patient's attention is drawn away from their own problems.[17]

Cody recently died, and after grieving the loss of my furry angel, I made sure to take the time to honor his life. I think I might finally be ready for a new furry friend. The void inside me is growing bigger and I recognize the necessity of having a pet to rub, snuggle, and love. I'm not the only one who recognizes the benefits from having a furry friend beside me. According to helpguide.com, studies have found that playing with a dog or cat can elevate levels of serotonin and dopamine, the neurotransmitters in the brain that calm and relax. They also report that dog owners are less likely to suffer from depression than those without pets. Makes perfect sense to me, that's for sure. And I think I'll name my new dog Valentina. It's inevitable that she'll steal my heart and be my every day Valentine.

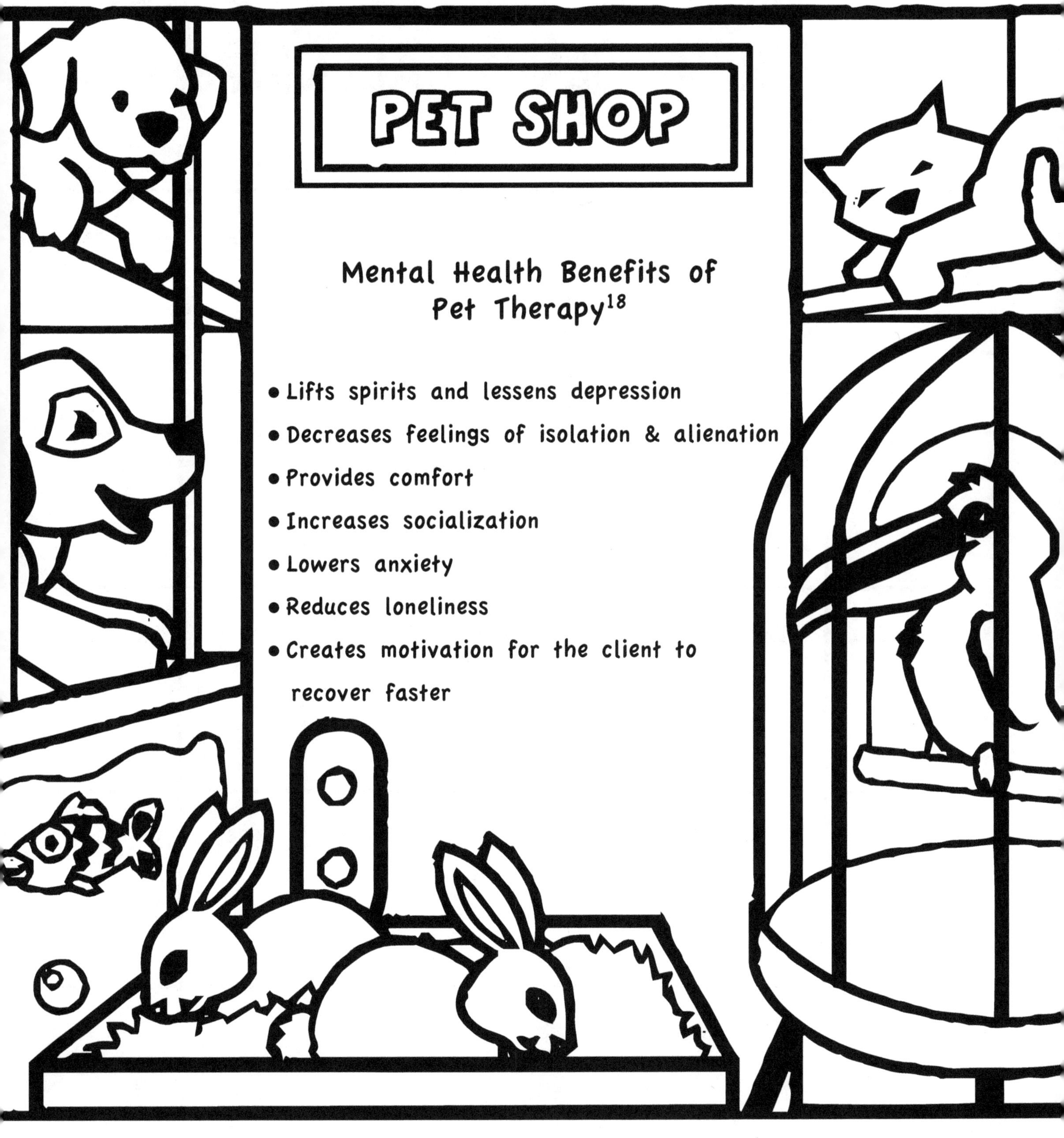
PET SHOP

Mental Health Benefits of Pet Therapy[18]

- Lifts spirits and lessens depression
- Decreases feelings of isolation & alienation
- Provides comfort
- Increases socialization
- Lowers anxiety
- Reduces loneliness
- Creates motivation for the client to recover faster

Even if you don't have a furry friend, there are many ways to spend time with a pet and get your dose of feel-good hormones.

Schedule time to spend with a friend's pet

FURRY FRIENDS CALENDAR

WEEK 1	Sunday	Monday	Tuesday	Wednesday	Thursday	Friday	Saturday
WEEK 2	Sunday	Monday	Tuesday	Wednesday	Thursday	Friday	Saturday
WEEK 3	Sunday	Monday	Tuesday	Wednesday	Thursday	Friday	Saturday
WEEK 4	Sunday	Monday	Tuesday	Wednesday	Thursday	Friday	Saturday

OR *Call your local animal shelters and volunteer.*

They are always looking for gentle, dedicated people to help with the animals.

	Activity	Website	Phone Number	Address	Hours to Commit	Notes
	Mike's Pet Shelter	*petshelter.com*	*777-777-7777*	*1234 S. Walnut*	*2-4pm*	Volunteers needed Mon & Wed to walk dogs. Apply online.
1.						
2.						
3.						
4.						
5.						

FURRY FRIEND REFLECTION

After spending time with my furry friend(s), I really enjoyed

I didn't like

My favorite part of the experience was

Next time I'm with my furry friend, I'm going to be sure to

because

At first I was concerned about

But now I feel

Reflect and journal anything else you're feeling about your experience

There's one more Incredible thing…

When we think of mental health disorders or mental illnesses, we often push back from the table. "That doesn't have anything to do with me," or "I'm not one of those people dealing with that kind of stuff" is what I often hear. Mental health challenges, or brain pain disorders, as I like to call them, are simply a function of our brains not being healthy. Our other organs get sick so why wouldn't our brains? We could potentially have knee, tooth and back pain just like we could have heart, kidney, and liver challenges, so it only makes sense that our brains would, at some point, need a checkup as well. And just like we would see a specialist for our different health issues, we should also see one for our brain pain; it directly impacts our health. Besides, mental health professionals have been trained to help us, and like I've said before, we're so worth it. No one deserves to live in pain or darkness.

When we talk about brain pain disorders, the good news is that there are symptoms that can be identified as well as causes and treatment options. And thanks to NAMI, the National Alliance on Mental Illness, we can access the most up-to-date information on brain pain disorders.

Here are some of the most common BRAIN PAIN DISORDERS...

BRAIN PAIN DISORDERS

SCHIZOPHRENIA

Schizophrenia is a serious mental illness that interferes with a person's ability to think clearly, manage emotions, make decisions and relate to others. It is a complex, long-term medical illness, affecting about 1% of Americans. Although schizophrenia can occur at any age, the average age of onset tends to be in the late teens to the early 20s for men, and the late 20s to early 30s for women. It is uncommon for schizophrenia to be diagnosed in a person younger than 12 or older than 40. It is possible to live well with schizophrenia.

Symptoms

It can be difficult to diagnose schizophrenia in teens. This is because the first signs can include a change of friends, a drop in grades, sleep problems, and irritability—common and nonspecific adolescent behavior. Other factors include isolating oneself and withdrawing from others, an increase in unusual thoughts and suspicions, and a family history of psychosis. In young people who develop schizophrenia, this stage of the disorder is called the "prodromal" period.

With any condition, it's essential to get a comprehensive medical evaluation in order to obtain the best diagnosis. For a diagnosis of schizophrenia, some of the following symptoms are present in the context of reduced functioning for a least 6 months:

Hallucinations. These include a person hearing voices, seeing things, or smelling things others can't perceive. The hallucination is very real to the person experiencing it, and it may be very confusing for a loved one to witness. The voices in the hallucination can be critical or threatening. Voices may involve people that are known or unknown to the person hearing them.

Delusions. These are false beliefs that don't change even when the person who holds them is presented with new ideas or facts. People who have delusions often also have problems concentrating, confused thinking, or the sense that their thoughts are blocked.

Negative symptoms are ones that diminish a person's abilities. Negative symptoms often include being emotionally flat or speaking in a dull, disconnected way. People with the negative symptoms may be unable to start or follow through with activities, show little interest in life, or sustain relationships. Negative symptoms are sometimes confused with clinical depression.

Cognitive issues/disorganized thinking. People with the cognitive symptoms of schizophrenia often struggle to remember things, organize their thoughts or complete tasks. Commonly, people with schizophrenia have anosognosia or "lack of insight." This means the person is unaware that he has the illness, which can make treating or working with him much more challenging.

Causes

Research suggests that schizophrenia may have several possible causes:

Genetics. Schizophrenia isn't caused by just one genetic variation, but a complex interplay of genetics and environmental influences. While schizophrenia occurs in 1% of the general population, having a history of family psychosis greatly increases the risk. Schizophrenia occurs at roughly 10% of people who have a first-degree relative with the disorder, such as a parent or sibling. The highest risk occurs when an identical twin is diagnosed with schizophrenia. The unaffected twin has a roughly 50% chance of developing the disorder.

Environment. Exposure to viruses or malnutrition before birth, particularly in the first and second trimesters has been shown to increase the risk of schizophrenia. Inflammation or autoimmune diseases can also lead to increased immune system

Brain chemistry. Problems with certain brain chemicals, including neurotransmitters called dopamine and glutamate, may contribute to schizophrenia. Neurotransmitters allow brain cells to communicate with each other. Networks of neurons are likely involved as well.

Substance use. Some studies have suggested that taking mind-altering drugs during teen years and young adulthood can increase the risk of schizophrenia. A growing body of evidence indicates that smoking marijuana increases the risk of psychotic incidents and the risk of ongoing psychotic experiences. The younger and more frequent the use, the greater the risk. Another study has found that smoking marijuana led to earlier onset of schizophrenia and often preceded the manifestation of the illness.

Treatment

There is no cure for schizophrenia, but it can be treated and managed in several ways.

Antipsychotic medications

Psychotherapy, such as cognitive behavioral therapy and assertive community treatment and supportive therapy

Self-management strategies and education

www.nami.org/Learn-More/Mental-Health-Conditions/Schizophrenia

DEPRESSION

Depression is more than just feeling sad or going through a rough patch. It's a serious mental health condition that requires understanding, treatment and a good recovery plan. With early detection, diagnosis and a treatment plan consisting of medication, psychotherapy and lifestyle choices, many people get better. But left untreated, depression can be devastating, both for the people who have it and for their families.

An estimated 16 million American adults—almost 7% of the population—had at least 1 major depressive episode last year. People of all ages and all racial, ethnic and socioeconomic backgrounds can experience depression, but it does affect some groups of people more than others. Women are 70% more likely than men to experience depression, and young adults aged 18–25 are 60% more likely to have depression than people aged 50 or older.

Getting a comprehensive evaluation is important. Underlying medical issues that can mimic a major depressive episode, side effects of other medications (like beta blockers or antihypertensives) or any other medical causes need to be ruled out. Understanding life stressors and prior responses to treatment effort can help shape a good treatment plan. Understanding how any co-occurring conditions fit into the diagnostic picture also informs treatment options.

Symptoms

Just like with any mental health condition, people with depression or who are going through a depressive episode (also known as major or clinical depression) experience symptoms differently. But for most people, depression changes how they function day-to-day.

Changes in sleep. Many people have trouble falling asleep, staying asleep or sleeping much longer than they used to. Waking up early in the morning is common for people with major depression.

Changes in appetite. Depression can lead to serious weight loss or gain when a person stops eating or uses food as a coping mechanism.

Lack of concentration. A person may be unable to focus during severe depression. Even reading the newspaper or following the plot of a TV show can be difficult. It becomes harder to make decisions, big or small.

Loss of energy. People with depression may feel profound fatigue, think slowly or be unable to perform normal daily routines.

Lack of interest. People may lose interest in their usual activities or lose the capacity to experience pleasure. A person may have no desire to eat or have sex.

Low self esteem. During periods of depression, people dwell on losses or failures and feel excessive guilt and helplessness. Thoughts like "I am a loser" or "the world is a terrible place" or "I don't want to be alive" can take over.

Hopelessness. Depression can make a person feel that nothing good will ever happen. Suicidal thoughts often follow these kinds of negative thoughts—and need to be taken seriously.

Changes in movement. People with depression may look physically depleted or they may be agitated. For example, a person may wake early in the morning and pace the floor for hours.

Physical aches and pains. Instead of talking about their emotions or sadness, some people may complain about a headache or an upset stomach.

How a person describes the symptoms of depression often depends on the cultural lens she is looking through. In Western cultures, people generally talk about their moods or feelings, whereas in many Eastern cultures, people refer to physical pain.

Causes

Depression does not have a single cause. It can be triggered, or it may occur spontaneously without being associated with a life crisis, physical illness or other risk. Scientists believe several factors contribute to cause depression:

Trauma. When people experience trauma at an early age, it can cause long-term changes in how their brains respond to fear and stress. These brain changes may explain why people who have a history of childhood trauma are more likely to experience depression.

Genetics. Mood disorders and risk of suicide tend to run in families, but genetic inheritance is only one factor. Identical twins share 100% of the same genes, but will both develop depression only about 30% of the time. People who have a genetic tendency to develop depression are more likely to show signs at a younger age. While a person may have a genetic tendency, life factors and events seem to influence whether he or she will ever actually experience an episode.

Life circumstances. Marital status, financial standing and where a person lives have an effect on whether a person develops depression, but it can be a case of "the chicken or the egg." For example, depression is more common in people who are homeless, but the depression itself may be the reason a person becomes homeless.

Brain structure. Imaging studies have shown that the frontal lobe of the brain becomes less active when a person is depressed. Brain patterns during sleep change in a characteristic way. Depression is also associated with changes in how the pituitary gland and hypothalamus respond to hormone stimulation.

Other medical conditions. People who have a history of sleep disturbances, medical illness, chronic pain, anxiety, and attention-deficit hyperactivity disorder (ADHD) are more likely to develop depression.

Drug and alcohol abuse. Approximately 30% of people with substance abuse problems also have depression.

Children and Teens

Children and teens. All children experience ups and downs while growing up, but for some, the downs aren't commonplace—they are symptoms of depression. Children and teens at higher risk for depression include those who have attention deficit/hyperactivity disorder, learning or anxiety disorders and oppositional defiance disorder. A young person who has experienced considerable stress or trauma, faced a significant loss or has a family history of mood disorders is at increased risk for depression.

Children with depression are more likely to complain of aches and pains than to say they are depressed. Teens with depression may become aggressive, engage in risky behavior, abuse drugs or alcohol, do poorly in school or run away. When experiencing an episode, teens have an increased risk for suicide. In fact, suicide is the third-leading cause of death among children aged 15-19.

Treatment

Although depression can be a devastating illness, it often responds to treatment. The key is to get a specific evaluation and a treatment plan. Today, there are a variety of treatment options available for people with depression.

Medications including antidepressants, mood stabilizers and antipsychotic medications

Psychotherapy including cognitive behavioral therapy, family-focused therapy and interpersonal therapy

Brain stimulation therapies including electroconvulsive therapy (ECT) or repetitive transcranial magnetic stimulation (rTMS)

Light therapy, which uses a light box to expose a person to full spectrum light and regulate the hormone melatonin

Exercise

Alternative therapies including acupuncture, meditation and nutrition

Self-management strategies and education

Mind/body/spirit approaches such as meditation, faith and prayer

www.nami.org/Learn-More/Mental-Health-Conditions/Depression

ANXIETY DISORDERS

Everyone experiences anxiety. Speaking in front of a group makes most of us anxious, but that motivates us to prepare and do well. Driving in heavy traffic is a common source of anxiety, but it keeps us alert and cautious to better avoid accidents. However, when feelings of intense fear and distress are overwhelming and prevent us from doing everyday things, an anxiety disorder may be the cause.

Anxiety disorders are the most common mental health concern in the United States. An estimated 40 million adults in the U.S., or 18%, have an anxiety disorder. Approximately 8% of children and teenagers experience the negative impact of an anxiety disorder at school and at home. Most people develop symptoms of anxiety disorders before age 21 and women are 60% more likely to be diagnosed with an anxiety disorder than men.

Symptoms

Anxiety disorders are a group of related conditions, and each with unique symptoms. However, all anxiety disorders have one thing in common: persistent, excessive fear or worry in situations that are not threatening. People can experience one or more of the following symptoms:

Emotional symptoms:

- Feelings of apprehension or dread
- Feeling tense and jumpy
- Restlessness or irritability
- Anticipating the worst and being watchful for signs of danger

Physical symptoms:

- Pounding or racing heart and shortness of breath
- Upset stomach
- Sweating, tremors and twitches
- Headaches, fatigue and insomnia
- Upset stomach, frequent urination or diarrhea

Types of Anxiety Disorders

Different anxiety disorders have various symptoms. This means that each type of anxiety disorder has its own treatment plan. The most common anxiety disorders include:

Panic Disorder

Characterized by panic attacks—sudden feelings of terror—sometimes striking repeatedly and without warning. Often mistaken for a heart attack, a panic attack causes powerful, physical symptoms including chest pain, heart palpitations, dizziness, shortness of breath and stomach upset.

Phobias

Everyone tries to avoid certain things or situations that make them uncomfortable or even fearful. However, for someone with a phobia, certain places, events or objects create powerful reactions of strong, irrational fear.

Generalized Anxiety Disorder (GAD)

GAD produces chronic, exaggerated worrying about everyday life. This can consume hours each day, making it hard to concentrate or finish routine daily tasks. A person with GAD may become exhausted by worry and experience headaches, tension or nausea.

Social Anxiety Disorder

Unlike shyness, this disorder causes intense fear, often driven by irrational worries about social humiliation–"saying something stupid," or "not knowing what to say." Someone with social anxiety disorder may not take part in conversations, contribute to class discussions, or offer their ideas, and may become isolated. Panic attack symptoms are a common reaction.

Causes

Scientists believe that many factors combine to cause anxiety disorders:

Genetics. Some families will have a higher than average numbers of members experiencing anxiety issues, and studies support the evidence that anxiety disorders run in families. This can be a factor in someone developing an anxiety disorder.

Environment. A stressful or traumatic event such as abuse, death of a loved one, violence or prolonged illness is often linked to the development of an anxiety disorder.

Treatment

As each anxiety disorder has a different set of symptoms, the types of treatment that a mental health professional may suggest also can vary. But there are common types of treatment that are used:

- Psychotherapy, including cognitive behavioral therapy
- Medications, including antianxiety medications and antidepressants
- Complementary health approaches, including stress and relaxation techniques

Read more about what specific treatment options are available on our treatment page.

www.nami.org/Learn-More/Mental-Health-Conditions/Anxiety-Disorders

BIPOLAR DISORDER

Bipolar disorder is a chronic mental illness that causes dramatic shifts in a person's mood, energy and ability to think clearly. People with bipolar have high and low moods, known as mania and depression, which differ from the typical ups and downs most people experience. If left untreated, the symptoms usually get worse. However, with a strong lifestyle that includes self-management and a good treatment plan, many people live well with the condition.

With mania, people may feel extremely irritable or euphoric. People living with bipolar may experience several extremes in the shape of agitation, sleeplessness and talkativeness or sadness and hopelessness. They may also have extreme pleasure-seeking or risk-taking behaviors.

People's symptoms and the severity of their mania or depression vary widely. Although bipolar disorder can occur at any point in life, the average age of onset is 25. Every year, 2.9% of the U.S. population is diagnosed with bipolar disorder, with nearly 83% of cases being classified as severe. Bipolar disorder affects men and women equally.

Symptoms

A person with bipolar disorder may have distinct manic or depressed states. A person with mixed episodes experiences both extremes simultaneously or in rapid sequence. Severe bipolar episodes of mania or depression may also include psychotic symptoms such as hallucinations or delusions. Usually, these psychotic symptoms mirror a person's extreme mood. Someone who is manic might believe he has special powers and may display risky behavior. Someone who is depressed might feel hopeless, helpless and be unable to perform normal tasks. People with bipolar disorder who have psychotic symptoms may be wrongly diagnosed as having schizophrenia.

Mania. To be diagnosed with bipolar disorder, a person must have experienced mania or hypomania. Hypomania is a milder form of mania that doesn't include psychotic episodes. People with hypomania can often function normally in social situations or at work. Some people with bipolar disorder will have episodes of mania or hypomania many times; others may experience them only rarely. To determine what type of bipolar disorder people have, doctors test how impaired they are during their most severe episode of mania or hypomania.

Although someone with bipolar may find an elevated mood appealing—especially if it occurs after depression—the "high" does not stop at a comfortable or controllable level. Moods can rapidly become more irritable, behavior more unpredictable and judgment more impaired. During periods of mania, people frequently behave impulsively, make reckless decisions and take unusual risks. Most of the time, people in manic states are unaware of the negative consequences of their actions. It's key to learn from prior episodes the kinds of behavior that signal "red flags" to help manage the illness.

Depression. Depression produces a combination of physical and emotional symptoms that inhibit a person's ability to function nearly every day for a period of at least two weeks. The level of depression can range from severe to moderate to mild low mood, which is called dysthymia when it is chronic.

The lows of bipolar depression are often so debilitating that people may be unable to get out of bed. Typically, depressed people have difficulty falling and staying asleep, but some sleep far more than usual. When people are depressed, even minor decisions such as what to have for dinner can be overwhelming. They may become obsessed with feelings of loss, personal failure, guilt or helplessness. This negative thinking can lead to thoughts of suicide. In bipolar disorder, suicide is an ever-present danger, as some people become suicidal in manic or mixed states. Depression associated with bipolar disorder may be more difficult to treat.

Early Warning Signs of Bipolar Disorder in Children and Teens

Children may experience severe temper tantrums when told "no." Tantrums can last for hours while the child continues to become more violent. They may also show odd displays of happy or silly moods and behaviors. A new diagnosis, Disruptive Mood Dysregulation Disorder (DMDD), was added to the DSM-5 in 2014.

Teenagers may experience a drop in grades, quit sports teams or other activities, be suspended from school or arrested for fighting or drug use, engage in risky sexual behavior or talk about death or even suicide. These kinds of behaviors are worth evaluating with a health care provider.

Causes

Scientists have not discovered a single cause of bipolar disorder. They believe several factors may contribute:

Genetics. The chances of developing bipolar disorder are increased if a child's parents or siblings have the disorder. But the role of genetics is not absolute. A child from a family with a history of bipolar disorder may never develop the disorder. And studies of identical twins have found that even if one twin develops the disorder the other may not.

Stress. A stressful event such as a death in the family, an illness, a difficult relationship or financial problems can trigger the first bipolar episode. Thus, an individual's style of handling stress may also play a role in the development of the illness. In some cases, drug abuse can trigger bipolar disorder.

Brain structure. Brain scans cannot diagnose bipolar disorder in an individual. Yet, researchers have identified subtle differences in the average size or activation of some brain structures in people with bipolar disorder. While brain structure alone may not cause it, there are some conditions in which damaged brain tissue can predispose a person. In some cases, concussions and traumatic head injuries can increase the risk of developing bipolar disorder.

Treatment

Bipolar disorder is treated and managed in several ways:

- Medications, such as mood stabilizers, antipsychotic medications and antidepressants
- Psychotherapy, such as cognitive behavioral therapy and family-focused therapy
- Electroconvulsive therapy (ECT)
- Self-management strategies and education
- Complementary health approaches such as meditation, faith and prayer

www.nami.org/Learn-More/Mental-Health-Conditions/Bipolar-Disorder

your very important notes

because you're worth it

Endnotes:

CHAPTER 1 - SUPPORT SQUAD

1. "Support Systems," *University of Michigan Depression Center: DepressionToolkit.org,* accessed October 23, 2016, http://www.depressiontoolkit.org/takecare/support_systems.asp

CHAPTER 2 – THERAPY

2. "Therapy," *Psychology Today,* Accessed October 23, 2016, https://www.psychologytoday.com/basics/therapy

CHAPTER 3 - HEALTHY BELLIES

3. Alli Contra, "Harvard Steps Up to the Healthy Eating Plate," *Food Safety News: Breaking news for everyone's consumption, accessed September 27, 2016,* http://www.foodsafetynews.com/2011/09/harvard-steps-up-to-the-plate/#.WHPBbWQrJPN
4. Oprah.com, "Your Vegan Shopping List," Oprah.com, accessed December 11, 2017 http://static.oprah.com/images/packages/vegan-starter-kit/vegan-shopping-list.pdf,
5. "Diet and Mental Health," *Mental Health Foundation, accessed September 9, 2016,* https://www.mentalhealth.org.uk/a-to-z/d/diet-and-mental-health

CHAPTER 4 – VISUALIZATION

6. "How To Be In Your Happy Place," *Wiki How To Do Anything,* accessed October 12, 2016, http://www.wikihow.com/Be-in-Your-Happy-Place

CHAPTER 5 - MEDITATION

7. "Benefits of Mindfulness: Practices for Improving Emotional and Physical Well-Being," *Helpguide.org: Trusted guide to mental, emotional and social health, accessed October 23, 2016,* http://www.helpguide.org/harvard/benefits-of-mindfulness.htm

CHAPTER 6 – EXERCISE

8. Kirstin Weir, "The Exercise Effect," *American Psychological Association,* December 2011, Vol 42, No. 11, http://www.apa.org/monitor/2011/12/exercise.aspx
9. "Exercise and Mental Health," *MindHealthConnect: Mental Health and Well Being, accessed October 23, 2016, https://www.mindhealthconnect.org.au/exercise-and-mental-health*

CHAPTER 7 - SLEEP

10. "Harvard Mental Health Letter: Sleep and Mental Health," *Harvard Health Publications Harvard Medical School: Trusted advice for a healthier life,* (July 2009), htty://www.health.harvard.edu/newsletter_article/Sleep-and-mental-health
11. "Harvard Mental Health Letter: Sleep and Mental Health," *Harvard Health Publications Harvard Medical School: Trusted advice for a healthier life,* (July 2009), htty://www.health.harvard.edu/newsletter_article/Sleep-and-mental-health

CHAPTER 8 - MUSIC

12. Darlene Oakley, "The Mental Health Benefits of Music," *EmpowHER: Improving Health. Changing Lives, accessed October 1, 2016,* http://www.empowher.com/emotional-health/content/mental-health-benefits-music?page=0,1
13. Darlene Oakley, "The Mental Health Benefits of Music," *EmpowHER: Improving Health. Changing Lives, accessed October 1, 2016,* http://www.empowher.com/emotional-health/content/mental-health-benefits-music?page=0,1

CHAPTER 9 - SOUL SERVICE

14. Kathy Gottberg, "Volunteering: 7 Big Reasons Why Serving Others Serves Us," *The Huffington Post:* (December 2014), http://www.huffingtonpost.com/kathy-gottberg/volunteering7-reasons-why_b_6302770.html
15. Sara Konrath, PHD, "How Volunteering Can Lessen Depression and Extend Your Life," Everyday Health, accessed September 21, 2016, http://www.everydayhealth.com/depression/how-volunteering-can-lessen-depression-and-extend-your-life.aspx

CHAPTER 10 - FURRY FRIENDS

16. "Therapy Pets and Humans with Mental Health Issues," *Dogtime.com,* accessed April 14, 2017, http://dogtime.com/dog-health/general/20839-pet-therapy-and-human-mental-health-issues.
17. "Therapy Pets and Humans with Mental Health Issues," *Dogtime.com,* accessed April 14, 2017, http://dogtime.com/dog-health/general/20839-pet-therapy-and-human-mental-health-issues.
18. "Benefits of Pet Therapy," *Paws for People: Healing Pet Therapy Since 2005,* Accessed April 14, 2017, http://www.pawsforpeople.org/who-we-are/benefits-of-pet-therapy/.

BRAIN PAIN DISORDERS:

- *NAMI, National Alliance on Mental Illness, Schizophrenia,* https://www.nami.org/Learn-More/Mental-Health-Conditions/Schizophrenia. Accessed December 2016
- *NAMI, National Alliance on Mental Illness, Depression,* http://www.nami.org/Learn-More/Mental-Health-Conditions/Depression. Accessed December 2016
- *NAMI, National Alliance on Mental Illness, Anxiety Disorders,* https://www.nami.org/Learn-More/Mental-Health-Conditions/Anxiety-Disorders. Accessed December 2016
- *NAMI, National Alliance on Mental Illness, Bipolar Disorder,* http://www.nami.org/Learn-More/Mental-Health-Conditions/Bipolar-Disorder. Accessed December 2016

Acknowledgements

This is for my Papa, Benjamin. I will love you always and enjoy feeling your pride on my shoulders. You never stopped believing in me, even when I didn't believe in myself. For that, and for so much more, I will love you into eternity.

Finding MY HAPPY has been the adventure of a lifetime. This journey has been made easier directly because of my TEAM HAPPY. I am incredibly moved by their support, encouragement, and overwhelming love in our mission to save the world.

TO MY TEAM HAPPY:

I am forever in HAPPY debt to my partner, Felecia, for being the absolute Yin to my Yang. We are kismet and the rest is us making Mental Fitness history and helping so many in need. Thank you for being an absolute flash of brilliance. I loved you from the second we shared air. And I will love you forever.

Thank you, Blondie (aka Mom), for being my bestest partner in crime. Team Happy wouldn't breathe beautiful life without you. Loving me through mental illness was a choice and one you made with grace.

Jamila, my JaJa and my market manager, hold on tightly because this is just the beginning. I'm indebted to you for your sisterhood and compassion and your acceptance of all my crazy.

There is no way I could ever be at my best (smile and all) without the unconditional support and encouragement from my living angel, Karlyn. I know I did something right to have been blessed by your love.

My Nikki... editor and overall overseer extraordinaire. You rock!

And my Old Lady Gang (Ilene, Michelle, Yolanda, June, Crystal), you are truly the bees knees. I am so honored and privileged to be led by your exceptional example. You are, indeed, gorgeous Golden Girls, and working beside you has been a fat dose of FABulous.

Thank you, Mary, for being the best godmother a girl from the south side of Chicago could ever have. I got lucky when God opened my eyes and you were there.

Reggae, you have been the mostest! When the world bestowed upon me the mentor of a lifetime, how did I know you would rock my Mental Fitness world? Let's dance all around in crimson and cream purpose.

My dear Gail, thank you for being the soul provider for my mission to impact hearts and save lives. Manifesting it ALL so we can be of sweet service to the human community is a journey I wake up early to experience with lots and lots and lots of oversized coffee mugs.

And the man behind the wheel, thank you, Lydell, for everything (read: making it happen in every part of these United States of America.) We drive to the ends of the world together – House music pumping – to reach those in need and we're always on time!

Uncle Kevin, the best mover and shaker this side of the Mississippi. This machine wouldn't turn without your grease. Thank you for being the connector.

Timothy, I couldn't have started the "Who Moved My Happy?" Movement without you. You have been my lifeline. And I will always be by your side – your true ride or die. Here's to us always making magic happen.

To my Dommy, my baby girl, sleeping on your floor when I was in a pinch so I could get to meetings and move the movement forward has been, in a word, PERF!

Simply put, thank you, Scott, for saving my little life.

The rest of my Team Happy, near and far, I am bowing down in gratitude for you. I make no mistakes about who is holding the net for those times when I fall. Thank you Dawn, Freddye, Gary, Aunt Tula, my filmmaker William, Mitchello, Noel, my Sands, my NYC sisters (Drenna, Rashana, Leah, Karen), Chris C., Ashley, Carmen V., Lauren, April, Arianne, Dr. Dawn Porter, my designer Tim Chapman, JoJo, Dr. Argie, Pamay, Nneka, Salim, Celeste, Toya Tate, and Antonise. I'm getting Tee Shirts with superhero capes sewn into the neckline and your names blazing across the front with lots and lots of sparkles.

♥

And to the colleges and universities that recognize the need for Mental Fitness, you are the real MVPs: Stanford University, Tennessee State University, Governors State University, Jackson State University, Alliance Ted K. Tajima and all the other schools and institutions that just get it and have added our Mental Fitness Movement to your team... thank you!

Deputy Chief of Staff to the Mayor, Vance Henry, and Former Special Assistant to the Governor, Terrance Hill, you are real rockstars!

Reshon, whenever my brain creates the next big thing in my lil world, you are the first to stand beside me and say, "Of course you can do that!" Words can't express how much that means to me. You are my Shero! Foreva and eva.

I will love you until the wheels fall off, Toya Rose, my first exercise in the unconditional.

Thank you to the American Foundation for Suicide Prevention (AFSP), The National Alliance on Mental Illness (NAMI), and the CIT (Crisis Intervention Teams) nationwide. Being able to work alongside your warriors has been life-changing.

I have the most amazing Mental Health Superstar Team in Jina, Margaret and Kevin Hines. Keep on keepin' on!

And to my Sisky Kristy, my Sunshine, thank you for being my one and only.

NOW, MOST IMPORTANTLY, TO YOU, THE READER:

I am wishing you patience and kindness as you move through this workbook adventure. You are the reason I exist and my life wouldn't make sense without you. I love you with my whole heart and you are so worth it – all of it! I'm beyond honored and privileged to walk with you in love and purity of heart. Be gentle with yourself and remember that your HAPPY is right here waiting for you! Just turn the page...

Erika is a Stanford University graduate with an MBA in marketing and international business. She is a former NBA cheerleader for the Chicago Bulls, a Random House author, and a Mental Fitness Junkie.

Website: erikajkendrick.com
Facebook: Erika Kendrick and Erika J. Kendrick
Instagram: @erikajkendrick
Twitter: @thecheerleaderE

CPSIA information can be obtained
at www.ICGtesting.com
Printed in the USA
FFHW022149210719
53712196-59434FF